D0946600

DATE DUE

30 505 JOSTEN'S			

Direct Approach

to

Counterpoint

in 16th Century Style

Direct Approach to Counterpoint

in 16th Century Style

By

GUSTAVE FREDRIC SODERLUND

[EASTMAN SCHOOL OF MUSIC SERIES]

PRENTICE-HALL, INC.

Englewood Cliffs, New Jersey

©1947
by PRENTICE-HALL, Inc.,
Englewood Cliffs, New Jersey

All rights reserved. No part of this book
may be reproduced in any form or by any means,
without permission in writing from the publisher.

Printed in the United States of America

ISBN: 0-13-214569-3

10 9 8 7 6 5 4 3

PRENTICE-HALL INTERNATIONAL, INC., *London*
PRENTICE-HALL OF AUSTRALIA, PTY. LTD., *Sydney*
PRENTICE-HALL OF CANADA, LTD., *Toronto*
PRENTICE-HALL OF INDIA PRIVATE LIMITED, *New Delhi*
PRENTICE-HALL OF JAPAN, INC., *Tokyo*

MT
55
.S68

Foreword

*D*irect *Approach to Counterpoint in Sixteenth-Century Style* by Gustave Fredric Soderlund is an important, authoritative, and illuminating addition to the list of textbooks on contrapuntal style. In accord with the best traditions of pedagogy the technical problems of sixteenth-century contrapuntal style are approached through a careful and exhaustive analysis of the music of the period, with special emphasis upon the works of Palestrina. By adopting this highly desirable approach the author avoids the sterility of academic strict counterpoint and initiates the student directly into the living art of the greatest of all contrapuntal periods.

The material presented in this text represents not only Mr. Soderlund's thorough and painstaking scholarship over many years of investigation but also embodies the practical results of his long career as a distinguished teacher of counterpoint. Thoroughly tested in the classrooms of the Eastman School of Music for the past twelve years, this text has proved to be highly valuable both to the composer and to the general student seeking an intimate knowledge of the fundamentals of sixteenth-century vocal polyphony.

Howard Hanson

Rochester, N. Y.

114929

Preface

The teaching of Counterpoint has for centuries past been confined to the system called Academic Counterpoint, embodied in the Five Species, first organized by Fux in his *Gradus ad Parnassum* (published 1725). The supposition by Fux that his system was based upon the contrapuntal practices of Palestrina cannot be maintained: the rigid adherence to a *cantus firmus* in even notes (already obsolete in the sixteenth century), and the exclusion, both of the ecclesiastical modes and of the rhythmical diversity of voice leading in the vocal polyphony, gives a highly artificial and stylistically misleading picture of the contrapuntal practice of the sixteenth century.

The homogeneous style found in the ecclesiastical compositions of the last half of the sixteenth century offers the best material for the study of contrapuntal practice, of which the treatment of dissonance is of especial importance. The greatest exponent of dissonance among the ecclesiastical composers may be found in Palestrina.

In this connection I refer, in grateful acknowledgment, to Knud Jeppesen's *The Style of Palestrina and the Dissonance*, a work of profound and brilliant scholarship, which has served as guide and inspiration for the writing of the present treatise.

The desirability of a direct approach to the style from a pedagogical standpoint was uppermost in my mind in the planning of this work. The hearing and the analysis of the music itself has been made the basis of procedure throughout. During the past twelve years the courses of Counterpoint in the Eastman School of Music have been conducted along these lines, with special emphasis upon choral performance of selected works of the period as well as of compositions written by the students. It was essential, from the beginning, that a volume of music be published which would give the students easy access to suitable material for analysis as well as for performance. This volume, *Examples of Gregorian Chant and Works by Orlandus Lassus, Giovanni Pierluigi Palestrina and Marc Antonio Ingegneri* is now the companion to *Direct Approach to Counterpoint in Sixteenth-Century Style*.

A debt of gratitude is due to the Director of the Eastman School of Music, Dr. Howard Hanson, whose sympathetic interest and suggestions made this work possible; to my graduate assistants for their most valuable help; to my colleagues in the Theory Department, Wayne Barlow, Allen I. McHose, Burrill Phillips, Donald White, for their interest and assistance in the teaching of the course. To Harold Gleason and Charles Warren Fox for helpful suggestions; to Rev. Benedict

Ehman and Rev. Wilfred Craugh of St. Bernard's Seminary for translations; and to the staff of the Sibley Library for their never failing courtesy.

Last, but not least, my warmest thanks go to my friend and editor, the late Professor Paul Weaver of Cornell University, whose patience and helpful advice have been of inestimable value in the preparation of the manuscript.

GUSTAVE FREDRIC SODERLUND

Rochester, N. Y.

Contents

PART ONE
THE CONTRAPUNTAL VOICE LINE

PART TWO
COUNTERPOINT IN TWO PARTS

PART THREE

COUNTERPOINT IN THREE PARTS

PART FOUR

COUNTERPOINT IN FOUR AND MORE PARTS

PART ONE

The
Contrapuntal Voice Line

Abbreviations

(Ex.):   The author's companion volume of music under the title
           *Examples of Gregorian Chant and Works by Orlandus Lassus, Giovanni
           Pierluigi Palestrina and Marc Antonio Ingegneri.*

L.:   Lassus.

P. 87, 4: Palestrina, page, and measure in Ex.
           References to music in the large collections: P. Vol. VII. 23. 1. 3.
           Volume, page, score, measure.

Chapter 1.

The Use of Modes · Musica Ficta · Cadences

THE USE OF MODES IN GREGORIAN CHANT

Tʜᴇ ancient Greek modal system from which the ecclesiastical modes were evolved was in use at the beginning of the Christian Era. We are not here concerned with the difference of conception between the ancient Greek system and that of the ecclesiastical modes; it is sufficient that the music itself presupposes a workable theory.

During the first centuries A.D. melodies were composed or adapted for use in the liturgy of the Christian Church. They then were known as *Musica, Cantilena,* or *Cantus.* These terms later were modified to *Cantus Planus* (plain chant, or plainsong). The main bulk of the chants was classified, and the four authentic modes and their plagal forms were adopted, presumably not later than the sixth century. They are traditionally known as Gregorian chant.

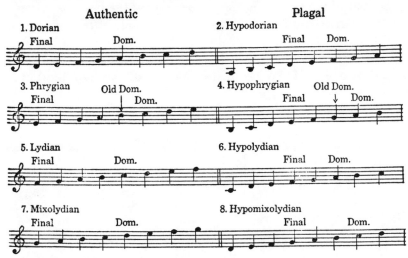

The numbering of the modes is in Roman tradition; in this treatise the Greek names of the modes will be retained.

The authentic and the plagal modes had the same final (the modern tonic), namely, the first degree of the authentic modes. The location of the dominant was subject to certain modifications due to the variable status of the note B. The melodic skip, direct or implied, of the tritone (from *tritonus,* meaning three whole tone steps) from F to B, causing an augmented fourth, was corrected by flattening B (the only accidental found in Gregorian chant). The modes affected were the

3

Phrygian (dominant on C), the Hypophrygian (dominant on A), and the Hypo-mixolydian (dominant on C). The remaining authentic modes all had their dominants on the fifth degree, and the remaining plagal modes had their dominants a third lower than those of the authentic modes.

The introduction of B flat brought about the actual, if not recognized, use of the two forbidden modes, the Aeolian and the Ionian; the former from the use of B flat in the Dorian mode, and the latter, for the same reason, in the Lydian mode.

One of the most interesting and important features of Gregorian chant is its rhythm. The Bible prose which furnished most of the texts was set in free and irregular rhythmical groups according to its meter. Only the elementary rhythms, i.e., twos and threes, were used. The tradition of this free rhythm is continued later in the polyphonic compositions of the fifteenth and the sixteenth centuries.

While modulation usually meant cadence, actual modulation was recognized. A perusal of some chants will show that change of mode, or key, attained a great degree of skill and subtlety. It was done, as in our day, by changing the center of the melodic line, i.e., the dominant (see Ex. chant 3).

From the ninth century onwards a simple notation called *neumes* was used. Gradually a staff was evolved which became standardized as a staff of four lines (ascribed to Guido d'Arezzo about the year 1000). The neumatic notation on a four-lined staff is still retained in chant books at the present time. Also available is a collection in modern notation, the *Liber Usualis*.

Gradually, with the advent and the development of polyphony, Gregorian chant fell into disuse. An attempt at simplification was made at the end of the sixteenth century which resulted in the publication of the Medici edition. Later research, begun in the latter part of the nineteenth century by the Monks of Solesmes, brought about a revival of the use of the chant and a true evaluation of its place in the realm of music.

THE USE OF MODES IN POLYPHONY

In the ecclesiastical vocal polyphony (and in the secular as well) the modes in actual use numbered twelve:

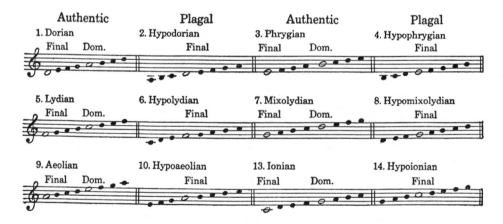

The eleventh and the twelfth modes, the Locrian and the Hypolocrian, were excluded, mainly due to cadential difficulties.

The authentic and the plagal forms of the modes used in Gregorian chant were, in practice, different scales with different dominants, although they had the same finals. *This distinction may be disregarded in polyphony;* the use of the two forms merely becomes a matter of range. In the perpendicular structure of polyphony the voices required room to move without too much crossing of parts; the distance between adjacent imitations became the conventional fifth or fourth (the range of an octave approximately divided in half); and the beginning of the composition usually expressed the mode by beginning on the final (tonic), or the dominant, with adjacent imitations at the fifth or the fourth. The last bass note of a composition, with a few exceptions, was the final of the mode. The range of the tenor part usually determined whether it was authentic or plagal: if between the final and its octave, it was authentic; if between the dominant and its octave, it was plagal. The range of both forms sometimes was extended as much as a third, upwards or downwards, or was extended in each direction, the total extension being that of a perfect fourth. In the latter case the mode was called mixed.

Occasionally the beginning of a composition does not express the mode. This is sometimes due to the use of plainsong themes beginning on notes other than those of the final or the dominant. The Kyrie of the Mass *De Feria* (P. Ex. 46), which is in the Phrygian mode, begins with an F which is often found as an initial note in the Hypophrygian mode in plainsong; the imitation is on C, with subsequent imitations on F and C. At first glance this would indicate the Lydian mode. The final cadence of the last Kyrie, however, is Phrygian.

TRANSPOSITION

Transposition a fifth down, or a fourth up, was commonly used. This transposition caused B flat to appear in the key signature, and E, corresponding to B in the untransposed modes, was lowered to avoid the tritone. This transposition was the only one in general use in ecclesiastical style.

Further transposition (by the student) may be easily effected through observing the degree in the C major scale on which each mode begins. For example, the Dorian mode, beginning, as it does, on the second degree of any major scale, will have the corresponding key signature of that scale. The student is advised to apply this procedure to all remaining modes in all major scales.

MUSICA FICTA

As we already know, only one accidental, B flat, was allowed in plainsong. During the evolution of polyphony several more accidentals were added: F sharp, C sharp, G sharp, and, in the transposed modes, E flat. It is true that other accidentals were known and occasionally used, but in ecclesiastical compositions their use was infrequent.

The accidentals did not always appear in the notation; they were applied by the choir, according to certain rules, a kind of *sub rosa* procedure which was called *musica ficta* (false or fictitious music).   By the application of these chromatics the cadence was made more convincing; the leading tone came into existence.   Probably the natural leading tones to the cadences on C and F showed the way.

CADENCES

Cadence (from *cadere*, to fall) means the formula which includes the immediate approach to a cadence point as well as the cadence point itself.   In plainsong this approach was usually made from above.   Later, in polyphony, a cadence in two parts was evolved: the approach to a cadence point by step from above in one of the parts and by step from below in the other, the step from below usually being raised in the case of F, C, or G.

The terms *modulation* and *cadence* were synonymous in plainsong as well as in polyphony.   Each mode had its specific cadence points, the use of which was generally adhered to.

A number of these cadences, however, were in common to most of the modes. This fact accounts for the vagueness (in the modern sense) of the specific modality during the course of a composition.   Modulation, understood as a change of key, did exist in plainsong, but in polyphony the original mode usually took over after the cadence.   There are, however, vague indications of a change of the harmonic center which might point to modulation in the modern sense.

The cadences listed for use in polyphony are in common for all forms of the modes.

From the melodic standpoint the fifth degree of the authentic modes is to be considered as the dominant.   From the harmonic standpoint, B is excluded as a cadence point and as a dominant.   The perpendicular harmonic element somewhat modified the importance of the dominant cadence and, instead, adopted the subdominant cadence in certain modes.   The Dorian, Lydian, Mixolydian, and Ionian modes preferred the fifth degree, while the Phrygian and the Aeolian preferred the fourth degree.   In the Phrygian mode a cadence on B was impossible because of the diminished triad, and the authentic cadence on E was impossible for the same reason.   In the Aeolian mode the fourth degree was preferred to the Phrygian cadence on E.

A list of cadence points in the different modes is found in Chapter 7.

Chapter 2.

Rhythm

Voice parts were not provided with barlines during the sixteenth century. There was a system of accentuation known as the greater, or Macro, rhythm which defined, in $\frac{4}{2}$ time, the first and third beats as strong, the second and the fourth beats as weak. The greater rhythm acted as a co-ordinator, or regulator, assigning the location of different devices, such as suspensions, cadences, and passing tones to certain beats. On the other hand, secondary, or Micro, rhythm was the irregular rhythmical grouping of each individual voice part. This system of irregular accentuation was inherited, of course, from plain chant. It was attained by the use of agogic accents, i.e., the juxtaposition of long note values to shorter ones. The use of barlines does not influence secondary rhythm; the agogic accents of each voice part occur on the longer note values and on any beat. The interplay of accents between the different parts, i.e., cross accents, creates the rich rhythmical life of the compositions of this age.

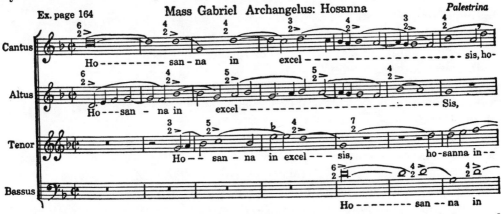

The foregoing excerpt illustrates these points. Metrical accents of the words should, as a rule, coincide with the musical accents. In case they do not, the musical accents predominate.

The student himself should now analyze secondary rhythm.

White notation was used, as a rule, during the sixteenth century. The white note values were five in number, the black note values, two.

Maxima Longa Brevis (breve) Whole note (semibreve) Half note (minim)

Quarter note (crotchet) Eighth note (quaver)

With barlines, the maxima is written as four tied breves, the longa as two tied breves. Unit of time was the half note, the whole note, and more rarely the dotted whole note.

Since we are committed to the use of the barlines, the way to use ties follows below:

Maxima   Longa   Dotted brevis   Brevis   Dotted whole note

Whole note   Dotted half   at the end of phrases or at the final cadence

The rules for ties are:

1. Equal white note values are tied to each other.

2. White note values are tied to half their value (corresponding to the dotted note).

3. Only adjacent note values are tied to each other.

4. Half notes may be tied to quarter notes, but quarter notes should not be tied to each other (there are very few exceptions).

5. Occasionally a whole note is tied to a breve at the end of a phrase, or at a final cadence.

6. Dotted whole notes occur on odd beats only.

By halving this notation and adding a few of the smaller note values we would have our present notation. It must be understood that the white notation does not indicate slow tempi. See Chapter 51 for further information.

In this treatise the white notation is used throughout. Practically all transcriptions in the great collections are in white notation; it is more practical to refer to contrapuntal usage in this notation than to have a double interpretation of the rules.

Time signatures will be limited to the ones most generally used during the sixteenth century: $\not\subset$ or $\frac{4}{2}$, ϕ or $\frac{3}{1}$ and $\frac{3}{2}$.

Few compositions use triple time throughout. The main bulk is written in $\frac{4}{2}$ time with occasional incursions in either $\frac{3}{1}$ or $\frac{3}{2}$ time. Within these limits there is more than sufficient scope for rhythmical diversity.

Later a brief reference will be made to the proportional system, inasmuch as the relation between the triple time and $\frac{4}{2}$ time will need further elucidation.

Chapter 3.

Melody

P<small>LAINSONG</small> as well as secular compositions furnished much of the thematic material for the vocal ecclesiastical compositions of the sixteenth century. The evolution of notation had brought about a more extended use of note values. The use of *musica ficta* caused the gradual elimination of the ecclesiastical modes and the later adoption of the modern major and minor modes and modulation.

A close relationship existed between the melodic intervals used in Gregorian chant and those of sixteenth-century ecclesiastical compositions, especially as regards Palestrina:

In Gregorian chant
    Frequently used
        Major and minor seconds, ascending and descending
        Major and minor thirds, ascending and descending
        Perfect fourths and fifths, ascending and descending
    Rarely used
        Major and minor sixths, ascending

In polyphony
    Frequently used
        Major and minor seconds, ascending and descending
        Major and minor thirds, ascending and descending
        Perfect fourths and fifths, ascending and descending
    Less frequently used
        Minor sixths, ascending only
        Perfect octaves, ascending and descending
    Rarely used
        Major sixths, ascending only

Augmented, diminished, and chromatic melodic intervals were forbidden except as *dead intervals* (interval relationship between the end of one phrase and the beginning of the next). The melodic tritone (from the Latin *tritonus*, three tones) between F and B was corrected by B flat or sometimes by F sharp. It is evident, however, that B flat was the favored chromatic as far as the tritone was concerned; F sharp is hardly ever found in Palestrina. The example below is exceptional; in order to have the final cadence chord complete the tenor skips from F sharp to B:

P. Vol. IV. 56. 4. 7-8.

It is interesting to note that the rarity of the B minor triad in the style may be directly attributed to the almost exclusive use of B flat to correct the tritone.

The following examples show the correction of the implied tritone:

P. Ex. 69, 18-20.

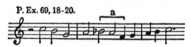

At a, the melody outlines the tritone, B and F being respectively the high and low tones at the point indicated.

P. Ex. 74, 31-34.

At b, F and B are accented, causing B to be flattened.

That the tritone was not always disliked is shown at c and d; here the harmonic background warrants the use of B natural. In general, each case should be judged on its own merits.

P. Ex. 87, 15-16.

P. Ex. 50, 71-74

Further chromaticism was limited to notes ascending to cadence points and to a change of the final chord of a cadence formula from minor to major. A detailed discussion of the matter will be found in Chapters 8, 9, 14, and 26.

Certain general characteristics are apparent in the contour of the melodic line. Stepwise motion is more prevalent than skips; their interrelated activity is extremely well balanced. An investigation of some of the purely technical aspects of the melodic line follows; most of the examples are taken from Palestrina.

Chapter 4 ·

Scalewise Passages

In GREGORIAN chant, scalewise passages up to seven notes may be found (see *Liber Usualis*, pp. 7, 673, 766), although they are more the exception than the rule. In the polyphony of the sixteenth century, however, scale passages up to an eleventh abound.

Scalewise passages in white notes only are not too frequent in more extended ranges:

Less extended passages of white notes in the same direction are very frequent; one of the most famous examples is found at the end of the Credo from *Pope Marcellus'* Mass, where descending passages of five white notes bring the final Amen to an overpowering, climactic close.

Chapter 5.

Single Skips

T HE general tendency is to approach and leave a skip in the opposite direction of the skip, by step or skip:

However, examples of skips, preceded or followed by motion in the same direction, are frequent enough to merit special attention:

Examples of the fifth, preceded and followed by step in the same direction, are extremely rare:

Of the foregoing examples of skips, approached and left in the same direction, that of the third occurs most frequently, while those of the fourth and fifth are very infrequent.

Of the minor sixth ascending, a very few instances of approach in the direction of the skip are found; it is not left by step in the same direction.

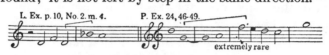

The octave may be preceded or followed by step in the same direction, but this occurs infrequently.

Chapter 6.

Two Skips in the Same Direction · Repeated Notes

Sᴋɪᴘs outlining the three notes of the major and the minor triads, the first and the second inversions, and the octave with the intervening fourth or fifth all occur in the style, the latter ones occurring mostly in the bass parts:

They normally should be approached and left in contrary motion, or by repetition of the first or the last note of the skips. The first note, however, may serve as the initial note of a phrase, or the last note as the final note. (The first note of a composition should not be smaller than a dotted half note.)

Instances of the exceptional usage of leaving ascending passages of two skips in the direction of the skips are quoted below:

The ascending skip of a perfect fifth followed by a minor third or, more rarely, by a major third is a favorite Dorian melodic idiom; the descending skip of a perfect fifth followed by a third is, on the other hand, quite infrequent. In practically all cases the sum of the two intervals is that of a minor seventh, which may be noticed in another combination of the two intervals, namely, the descending minor third followed by the perfect fifth:

Two perfect fourths or two perfect fifths in the same direction are permitted in long note values only; such occurrences, however, are quite rare:

REPEATED NOTES

Long note values are often divided into smaller units of time. They are sometimes of equal value, but are more often unequal in order to create diversified rhythm. In homophonic style which often occurs in the longer movements of the Mass, i.e., the Gloria and the Credo, repeated notes are very frequent; they are not limited to any particular movement, but may occur anywhere. The number of repeated notes should not be too large; the author has found no more than seven. An even greater number is found, however, in compositions of purely declamatory character, such as the Improperia (see P. Vol. XXXI p. 176).

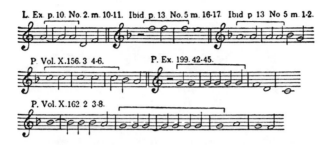

Chapter 7.

Preliminary Exercises in Melody Writing in White Note Values Without Text

For the preliminary exercises only white note values are to be employed.

For the use of tied notes, see Chapter 2. Ties of longer duration may occur occasionally as a result of augmentation or the use of a pedal at the end of a composition (see Ex. 73, 75, 93–122, 185–213). In such cases whole notes are tied to breves; this may also occur at the end of a phrase, or at the end of a composition.

Do not tie dotted notes to other note values in ₵, or $\frac{4}{2}$ time. Observe that, as a rule, only adjacent note values are tied. The procedure in $\frac{3}{1}$ or $\frac{3}{2}$ time will be taken up later. For the present, all melody writing will be confined to $\frac{4}{2}$ time. The unit of time, or beat, is a half note.

The initial theme of a composition always begins on the first beat; interior phrases may begin on any beat. All through the style a kind of law of momentum is observed, especially at the beginning of a composition; the melody gathers speed, as it were.

Punctuation of the melody is done by cadences and sometimes by rests. The following * are the cadences, in order of their importance, in general use in polyphony in common for both the authentic and the plagal forms of the modes:

	Common	*Infrequent*	*Rare*
Dorian	D A F	G C	E
Phrygian	E A G	D C	F
Lydian	F C A	D	
Mixolydian	G D C	A	F E
Aeolian	A D C	G F	E
Ionian	C G A	D	F E

* My findings on this point agree exactly with those of Jeppesen except in the case of the Lydian mode.
G. F. S.

The student should write melodic phrases of about six measures in length, ending on a cadence point. The cadence point, in two-part counterpoint, was practically always approached by step from above or below. When approached from below, F, C, and G were raised a half step. The cadence point on A was occasionally approached from above by B flat, in which case G remained natural (Phrygian cadence), and the one on E, the true Phrygian cadence point, was approached from above by F and from below by D. No accidentals in this case!

In practice, each voice part was written within its own range. Hence, the problem of choosing between the authentic or plagal forms of the mode need not bother the student. There is, however, another problem of importance connected with writing for voices, that of *tessitura*, also called "heart of the range." The term refers to the position of the notes in a voice part. For example, in some vocal compositions the melody may remain persistently in the highest register of the voice for a considerable time: the tessitura is then said to be high.

It is timely here to quote an excerpt from a pamphlet issued by the American Academy of Singers regarding the subject of tessitura:

It is common knowledge that a great many teachers of singing hesitate to permit their pupils to participate in choral singing because experience has proven that due to the unusually high tessitura dominating the arrangements of many choral works, harm is done to the voice.

The subject of tessitura involves certain basic facts pertaining to the safe use of the singing voice. These, in the opinion of many teachers, have been, and continue to be widely misunderstood and frequently disregarded by composers, arrangers, and publishers. In order to clarify the basic principles involved, and their practical application, the following beliefs are presented which have been reached through prolonged application and study, and confirmed by experience.

In this connection the designation tessitura, or "heart of the range," is used in accordance with the definition given by Grove's Dictionary as "the prevailing or average position of the notes in relation to the compass of the voice, whether high, low or medium," and is not to be confused with the word range. In the following tabulations the vocal limits allocated to the various voices are those of the average amateur singer and not of the professional artist, and refer only to choral music.

A dangerously high tessitura is apt to strain and even permanently injure young and adolescent voices and prevent normal development of the vocal apparatus.

The best range and the safest and best tessitura for the various voices are as follows:

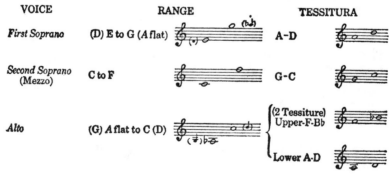

First Tenor	(D) E to F sharp (G)		A-D
Second Tenor	(C) D to E (F)		F#-C
Baritone	A to D		D-A
Bass	(E) F to B (C)		(2 Tessiture) Upper-Eb-Ab / Lower F-Bb

The tessitura limitations do not prohibit the composer and arranger from writing for the full range of the voice. *

The following are the voice ranges in compositions of the vocal polyphonic period:

Cantus (Soprano)   Alto   Tenor   Bass

The two tabulations show a slight difference in the main classes of voices in regard to range. The tessitura, however, is high on an average, especially in the tenor parts. Some bass parts are high enough for baritones (see P. Ex. *Exaltabo Te*, p. 177). This is due to conditions peculiar to the period.

The church choirs were not very large (the membership probably not exceeding thirty). Their members were selected with care from those with the best available training; their excellence is reflected in the vocal ranges of the music for it is evident that the composers were writing for professional singers.

The student should use extreme care in the matter of range. Write for average voices, always remembering that the lowest tones are weak, and that extremes of range should be used sparingly. A melody should not have too many high or low points; a well-balanced melody reaches one high point and, generally, does not return to it in the same phrase.

The exercises on the following page are modifications of thematic material in *Examples*. Until the student is thoroughly familiar with secondary rhythm, the exercises should be written both with and without barlines.

The following points should be kept in mind:

1. Begin on the first beat with a whole note or larger note value. To express the mode, use the following notes as initials in the different modes:

Dorian: D or A
Phrygian: E, A, or B
Lydian: F or C
Mixolydian: G or D
Aeolian: A or E
Ionian: C or G

* Permission to reprint this quotation has been granted by Mr. Homer G. Mowe.

2. There should be a judicious balance between stepwise motion and skips; stepwise motion occurs more frequently. In general, approach and leave skips in the opposite direction. The various examples of skips in white notes which do not follow this rule, and also two skips in the same direction, should be thoroughly studied.

3. The skip of the augmented fourth or the diminished fifth must be corrected by flattening B.

4. Secondary rhythm is a feature of the style. The agogic accents (accents by duration) should occasionally be placed on even beats; when on the fourth beat, by tying notes over the barline. Avoid a too regular rhythmical scheme.

5. Learn the table of cadence points. They should be approached from above or below by step; when approached from below, the following notes should be raised; F, C, and G. The cadence point A may be approached from above by B flat, in which case the G is not altered. The true Phrygian cadence point on E is approached from above by half step and from below by whole step; remember, no accidentals in this case!

6. The cadence points always occur on the odd beats; for the time being they should be approached from below by a half note value and from above by a whole note value.

7. It is not necessary to consider the melodies from the authentic or the plagal viewpoint; but it is necessary to consider them from the viewpoint of voice range.

8. Always indicate, at the beginning of the melody, the voice for which it is intended. Learn to write a neat manuscript. Stems should be kept within the staff in one-part writing:

9. Sing your own exercises; if the melody is too hard to sing, it probably is poorly done.

10. Learn the modes by singing, as well as by playing them on your particular instrument. Transpose them to all keys.

Write exercises using white note values and secondary rhythm. End on a cadence point.

PART TWO

Counterpoint
in Two Parts

Chapter 8.

Counterpoint in Two Parts · Note Against Note

COUNTERPOINT, from the Latin *punctus contra punctum* (a reference to the shape of the notes of early notation), is the art of combining melodies; a theme is provided with a counter-subject, or counterpoint, above or below. It may be done as imitation, or as free counterpoint.

The vertical intervallic relationship between two melodic lines is based on consonance. The consonances were:

Unison	perfect
Fifth	perfect
Octave	perfect
Third	major and minor
Sixth	major and minor

The perfect fourth was a dissonance in the style (except in the special case of the *consonant* fourth which will be considered in Chapter 37).

Augmented and diminished intervals were forbidden. Harmonic analysis is done from beat to beat by measuring the distance from the lowest pitched note to the note above.

Exercises in two-part writing, note against note:

(The double G clef for the tenor part indicates that it should be read an octave lower.)

The foregoing examples illustrate the simplest relationship between the horizontal melodic and the vertical harmonic concepts; two adjacent voices, soprano and alto, or tenor and bass, showing independent melodic lines and a vertical intervallic structure. The cadence point D in the first example is approached by step from above and below, with customary chromatic alteration. The cadence

23

point E is approached in the same manner except for the chromatic alteration; **this** is the Phrygian cadence, approached by half step from above and by whole step from below. The approach, by step from above and below, to the final cadence point was called *clausula vera* (true cadence). The same procedure was used for the other cadence points; different names were given to them according to their location. In two parts, the true cadence is the most useful of the cadence formulas, especially in combination with the 7–6 and the 2–3 suspensions.

These are the basic formulas for the cadences in two parts:

Specific rules:

1. Unisons should be used only at the beginning and at the end; they should be approached and left by contrary motion.

2. Fifths should be approached by contrary motion; more rarely by step in the upper and skip in the lower part.

3. Octaves should always be approached by contrary motion.

4. Parallel thirds and sixths should, for the time being, be limited to three in succession.

5. As a rule, use close position. Occasionally a compound interval may occur.

6. In the crossing of parts the low note will be that of the upper part, and the high note that of the lower part.

7. Always write each voice part on a separate staff.

Some of these rules will be modified later; they apply only to note against note writing in two parts.

Exercises should now be written in all modes. First write a theme in even white note values. End the theme on the final cadence point. Add a counterpoint, either above or below. Write the numbers of the harmonic intervals above the low part.

Chapter 9.

Two Notes Against One . Consonances Only

USE CONSONANCES ONLY

THE rules given in the previous chapter are still in force, except that of the unison: the second of two half notes may be a unison provided that it occurs on one of the even beats against a note of at least double its value. The fifth and the octave are approached in contrary or oblique motion, by skip or step.

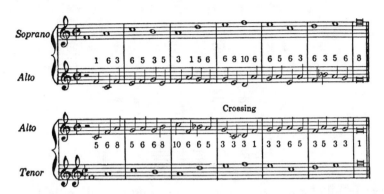

It is undesirable to have the unaltered B appear too near the cadence point F. The sixteenth-century composers avoided the pure Lydian mode because of the difficulty in getting cadence on the final. Palestrina, in the few cases of his use of the pure Lydian mode, invariably uses A as the final (see Ex. 76).

In the first example above, the B flat serves two purposes: it corrects the melodic tritone and makes the cadence sound more convincing.

Write several exercises in different modes, with the counterpoint above as well as below. End with clausula vera.

Chapter 10.

The Half Note Passing Tone

THERE are two kinds of passing tones: the diatonic and the chromatic; the style requires only the diatonic.

The diatonic passing tone is approached and left by step in the same direction. It abridges the melodic interval of a major or a minor third, is unessential, or non-harmonic, in character, and is consequently dissonant.

The half note passing tone is restricted to the second or the fourth beats in $\frac{4}{2}$ time. For this reason it will be considered as unaccented (the difference between accented and unaccented passing tones will be explained in Chapter 24). It may ascend or descend, always against double or more of its value.

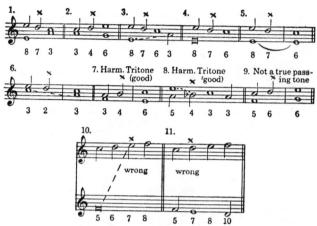

Examples 1–8 illustrate ascending and descending half note passing tones on beats two or four. In example 9, D is a consonance; hence, not a true passing tone. In example 10, the passing tone is on the wrong beat. In example 11, a passing tone is attempted on the second beat; the basic harmony, on the first beat, however, should not have changed; the dissonance on beat two is consequently disallowed.

Half notes are not used as lower auxiliaries except in the diminution triple time. They are never used as upper auxiliaries. Upper and lower auxiliaries occur as quarter notes or eighth notes on the off beats only. They are approached and left by step.

Skips to or from dissonant harmonic intervals are forbidden (1). But the note opposite that of a dissonant passing tone may skip, provided that it skips to a consonance (2):

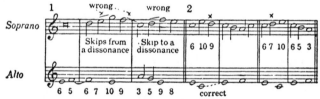

All white note values may now be used. The counterpoint may begin simultaneously with the theme, or it may enter after one or more beats.

Rests corresponding to white note values are:

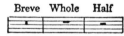

Secondary rhythm should be practiced in every exercise. In order to be constantly aware of this important phase of the technique, the rhythm should be marked in every part until facility is attained. Notice the cross rhythm:

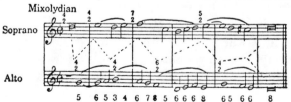

Chapter 11.

Suspensions in $\frac{4}{2}$ Time

T HE principal dissonance in sixteenth-century composition is the suspension. It is produced by arresting the stepwise downward movement of one or more of the parts in a progression while the other part or parts move to their place in the chord. In two parts a progression of two consonant intervals forms the basic material:

The 7–6 and its inversion, the 2–3, are the most effective in two parts. They may be used anywhere in the texture, and at cadences exclusively, their resolutions, the sixth and the third, forming the initial cadence chord of the clausula vera type of cadence.

The 4–3 suspension is rarely used in two parts, and the 9–8 suspension even more rarely because of its ineffective resolution to the empty octave. The 7–6 and the 4–3 are suspensions *above*, the resolution occurring above the low voice, and the 2–3 suspension *below*, the resolution occurring in the lowest voice.

The suspension formula recognizes three phases:

1. Preparation (consonance) on beats two or four.
2. Suspension (dissonance) on beats one or three.
3. Resolution (consonance) on beats two or four.

The formula usually occupies three time units (half note beats). The resolution *always* occurs on the beat immediately following the suspension beat. Both the preparation and the resolution beats may be two units of time if necessary, but the suspension is always limited to one beat. *The resolution is always stepwise downward.*

(Compare with the previously given basic material.)

The part of the suspension in which the resolution occurs will be recognized as a *suspension melody:*

Write a number of basic progressions; then use them for suspension formulas. Also write exercises in two parts using suspensions in the texture as well as at the cadence. Continue to use white note values only.

Chapter 12.

Imitation

IMITATION is a repetition in one voice of a theme previously stated in another voice at a certain intervallic distance above or below. The imitation following closely upon the beginning of the theme is said to be in stretto, a device commonly used in the sixteenth century. Any intervallic relationship was used, provided it was diatonic; in general, however, adjacent voices imitated each other at the fourth or the fifth (see Chapter 3).

Imitation is strict (canon), or free. The canon, eldest form of imitation, originated with the composers of the thirteenth century. It was later known as *Caccia* (hunt) in Italy in the fourteenth century, and *Fuga* (flight) in the fourteenth and fifteenth centuries.

The imitation is strict, note for note, although not always interval for interval. The initial theme is called *Dux*, or leader, or antecedent, and the imitation, *Comes*, or follower (literally, *companion*), or consequent. The canon is interrupted at the end and a short coda (tail) is added leading to a cadence.

Two (voices) *in one* (canon) is the term given to a canon in two parts; *three* (voices) *in one* (canon), a three-part canon; *four* (voices) *in two* (canons), two simultaneous two-part canons. A composition in three or more parts may have a two- or three-part canon running through it, while the other part or parts are in free imitation (see P. Ex. 61, 73).

Free imitation repeats the beginning of the theme note for note up to a certain point. This kind of imitation is the most frequently found in the sixteenth century; the scope of imagination was not hindered by the shackles of the strict imitation.

The following devices are in common for both canonic and free imitation:

1. *Mirroring* (also called *inversion*) in which ascending and descending movement is reversed in the imitation (for example, an ascending third becomes a descending third in the imitation). See P. Ex. 76.

(See also P. Ex. 51.)

2. *Augmentation* imitates in note values twice as large, or more (see P. Ex. 71):

(See also P. Ex. 84, and P. Ex. 93–122.)

3. *Diminution* is the opposite of augmentation; the note values are halved in the imitation. The device is infrequent. An example may be found in Palestrina's *Missa Brevis*, at the end of the first Kyrie, between the soprano and the tenor.

There is, however, what may be termed free diminution, as well as augmentation, in which the contour of the theme is preserved but the note values changed in various ways:

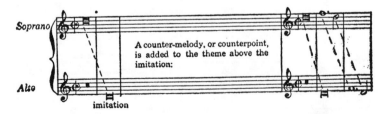

Ky - ri-e - e - lei - - son   Ky - ri-e e-lei - - - son

The example above is taken from the Mass *Ut Re Mi Fa Sol La* (P. Ex. 185) which offers a number of other variations. Often augmentation, or diminution, is applied to the initial note of a theme (see P. Ex. 24, 27).

4. *Per recte et retro* (forward and backward): the theme is imitated backwards. It is sometimes called *Cancrizans* (crab). Its musical value is doubtful.

Real imitation answers the theme interval for interval (in the diatonic sense: perfect intervals answer perfect intervals, but major intervals may be answered by minor, and minor by major).

In *Tonal* imitation the note of the final is answered by that of the dominant, and the note of the dominant by that of the final; the object is to establish tonality. A modification of the answer follows as a matter of course (see P. Ex. 22, 27). Tonal imitation is comparatively infrequent in the style; the sixteenth-century composers preferred the real answer.

Chapter 13.

Imitation in Two Parts . White Note Values Only

Continue to use white note values (with the exception of dotted halves). Practice the use of consonance only, in the first exercises.

Examples of imitation in all modes at all simple diatonic intervals above as well as below, beginning with the octave:

Dorian. Imitation at the octave below.

The exercise continues in this fashion until a suitable cadence point is reached (for the present always the final):

By changing the rhythm of the last measure in the previous exercise a suspension has been added:

In the foregoing example the imitation is strict until the penultimate measure. As a general rule the imitation in two parts is conducted to as near the cadence as possible.

The 7–6, 2–3, and 4–3 suspensions should now be used, as well as the half note passing tone; before the final cadence only 7–6 and 2–3 are suitable.

Dorian. At the seventh below:

As a general rule, themes beginning on the odd beats were imitated on the odd beats, and those beginning on the even beats, on the even (the latter in interior phrases only). A change of imitation beats, from one to three or from two to four, promoted cross accents (see Chapter 11).

Ionian. At the sixth above:

The imitation may begin on a suspension dissonance.

Mixolydian. At the fifth below:

3 5 6 8 | 10 6 3 3 | 3 5 6 5 | 4 3 5 3 | 2-3 1

When the initial cadence chord in the final cadence occurs on beat two and the final on beat three, the whole note of the final is tied to a breve in the last measure.

Aeolian. At the fourth above:

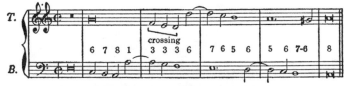

crossing
6 7 8 1 | 3 3 3 6 | 7 6 5 6 | 5 6 7-6 | 8

Since the remaining imitation intervals are smaller than the fourth and the fifth (the difference in range between adjacent voices), it is convenient, in order to avoid range difficulties, to use a pair of voices of the same denomination.

Mixolydian. At the third below:

crossing
6 5 | 3 4 5 6 | 6 5 3 1 | 3 5 3 3 | 3 5 6 3 | 2 3 2-3 | 1

Dorian. At the second below:

crossing
3 4 5 6 | 5 6 6 5 | 3 1 3 4 | 3 3 3 4 | 6 6 7-6 | 8

Phrygian. At the unison:

crossing
3 1 8 3 | 2 3 3 5 | 6 8 3 3 | 3 3 2-3 | 1

In imitations at the third, the second, and the unison, a discreet use of crossing is recommended as a means of maintaining good balance of the melodic line (see P. Ex. 166, the canon between the two altos). When imitating at the unison it is generally best to avoid using too close a stretto. Always observe the cardinal rule of contrapuntal style: *movement* against stationary note values.

Exercises should now be written in all modes and at all simple intervals, the imitations above as well as below. Pay special attention to secondary rhythm.

Chapter 14.

Scalewise Quarter Notes in the Melodic Line

QUARTER notes in scalewise passages preceded and followed by white note values:

Both ascending and descending forms are frequent:

Pairs between white note values should, as a rule, occur on weak beats:

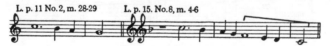

The ascending form preceded by note values larger than a half note should not be attempted; the following were not used:

But after a half note, quarter note pairs are quite common in both ascending and descending forms:

Pairs on the strong beat, between white notes, should be avoided except in certain melodic idioms; they often precede and lend emphasis to the preparation of the suspension:

The following should be avoided altogether both in conjunct and disjunct motion because of its rhythmical rigidity; it is not found in the style:

Further use of scalewise passages is shown in the following examples. The largest number found is eight ascending and nine descending:

Interior phrases frequently begin with quarter notes on the strong or the weak beat after a rest, or immediately following a preceding phrase. The number should always be even — from four to ten; pairs have not been found. The few examples of a single quarter note preceded by a quarter rest (P. Ex. 78, 61) are hardly sufficient to establish stylistic usage.

Chapter 15.

Stepwise Use of Quarter Notes with Change of Direction • Sequences

CHANGE of direction offers a wider scope in the projection of the melodic line. Some representative examples are quoted, among which a few infrequent idioms are included:

Students are advised to look up other forms for themselves.

SEQUENCES

A few instances of melodic sequences are quoted below. They are extremely rare in the style (especially the last example).

Chapter 16.

Skips in Quarter Notes · The Nota Cambiata

THE term *Nota Cambiata* is derived from the Italian verb *cambiare*, to change. The Nota Cambiata (literally, *changed note*) was a favorite melodic idiom before and during the sixteenth century. The archaic form consisted of three notes; the sixteenth-century version, the classical Nota Cambiata, has four notes.

The Cambiata may be explained as an intended passing note figure with a change of direction; the second note skips downward a third, followed by an ascending step to the final note, the intended goal of the quarter note passing tone. It may be placed on any beat; it is extremely rare on the initial beat of a composition. It is found in all voice parts.

The fourth note is generally followed by ascending stepwise motion, i.e., in the direction of the last notes of the figure. Downward progressions are rare. As seen from the examples, the fourth note may have the value of a half note, a dotted half, a whole note, or a breve, and it is sometimes raised chromatically:

Type 1

A very effective use of the Cambiata is sometimes found at a final cadence; the fourth note is then a member of the final cadence chord:

Type 2

No note values in this figure are changed. The direction from the last note is consistently upwards:

The faster tempo of the diminuted triple time actually reduces the following figure to half value, i.e.,  (Type 2):

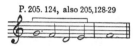

Type 3

This is the least frequent of the Cambiatas:

Chapter 17.

Skips from Half Notes to Stepwise Quarter Note Passages

THE skip is nearly always made from a half note value:

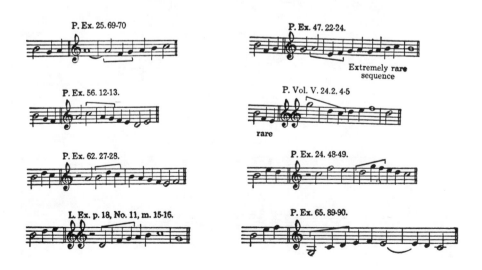

Chapter 18.

Skips from Stepwise Quarter Note Passages to White Note Values

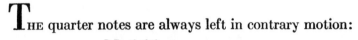

The quarter notes are always left in contrary motion:

L. Ex. p. 15, No. 8, m. 10-12.

L. Ex. p. 17, No. 10, m. 3-5.

P. Vol. V. 52. 2.5

Chapter 19.

Quarter Note Skips Followed by White Note Values

THE skips are always descending. The first quarter note is sometimes tied to a preceding half note. The skip is always succeeded by motion in the opposite direction, except that of the third, which may be followed by motion in the same direction as that of the skip:

L. Ex. p. 17, No. 10, m. 16-17

P. Ex. 127, 50-51

P. Ex. 32, 79

P. Ex. 22, 8-9

P. Ex. 26, 79

L. Ex. p. 11-12, No. 3, m. 18-19

Chapter 20.

Quarter Note Figures with Skips

Sₖɪₚₛ between quarter notes were subject to a restriction called the *high note law*. It may be briefly described thus: The high note of an ascending skip was generally felt as an accent; since all accents fell on the first half of the beat, an ascending skip from a quarter note on the first half of the beat to the second half of the beat was avoided in order not to cause an accent on the off beat:

This is especially the case in Palestrina; the concept is quite general, however, in other composers in the sixteenth century. Exceptions may be found in all of them, but these are not frequent enough to establish the usage as part of the style. Two quarter note skips in the same direction are extremely rare and should not be attempted by the student.

A variation of the figure with two skips in the same direction in white note values may be noted:

After the skips the figure is continued in quarter notes.

Subsequent quarter note figures may occur on any beat in the measure; the first note of the figure must be on the beat.

---

* See Jeppesen: *The Style of Palestrina and the Dissonance*, p. 58; ———: *Counterpoint*, translated by Glen Hayden, p. 87.

1. A stepwise approach of two or more quarter notes to a high point, followed by a descending skip of a third, a fourth, a fifth, or an octave:

If the last two notes of the figure occur on beats one or three they are frequently followed by a dotted half or a whole note. This is generally observed in the use of any quarter note figures, especially when they occur in pairs.

2. The second note of the figure is approached by an ascending step followed by a downward skip of a third, a fourth, or a fifth. Number 6 is extremely rare; it is found in *Cantiones Sine Textu.*

3. The Nota Cambiata sometimes occurs in quarter notes, although not so frequently as the classical Cambiata.

4. A stepwise descending figure of three quarter notes followed by a descending skip of a third or a fourth. The first quarter note is frequently tied to a preceding half note.

5. A lower auxiliary figure followed by a downward skip of a third.   More extended skips have not been found.

6. Two descending stepwise quarter notes followed by an ascending skip of a third or a fourth, the skip followed by stepwise motion in the opposite direction. Number 14, a similar figure with stepwise motion in the direction of the skip, is less frequent.

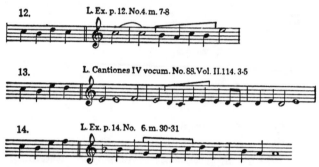

The ascending skips of a fifth and an octave have not been found.

7. *a*) A descending skip of a third followed by stepwise motion in the opposite direction.

b) The same followed by an ascending step with stepwise change of direction.

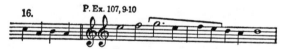

c) The same followed by an ascending step and a descending skip of a third or a fourth.

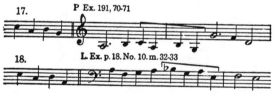

d) The same followed by an ascending skip of a third and a descending step.

e) The same followed by an ascending skip of a third and an ascending step.

f) The same followed by an ascending skip of a fourth and a step in the opposite or the same direction.

g) The same followed by an ascending skip of an octave and a descending step.

8. A descending skip of a fourth, fifth, or an octave:

Number 24 followed by stepwise motion in the opposite direction;

Number 25 followed by skip of an octave and a step in the opposite direction;

Number 26 followed by stepwise motion in the opposite direction;

Number 27 followed by a skip of a third in the opposite direction and an ascending step in the same direction.

Chapter 21.

Quarter Notes and Eighth Notes Combined in the Melodic Line

EIGHT notes occur in groups of two on the second half of the beat and consequently may be preceded by either a dotted half note or a quarter note. They are approached and left by stepwise motion, and the eighth notes are also stepwise.

1. In a scale line, descending or ascending:

2. The first note as a lower auxiliary:

3. The second note as a lower auxiliary, with a descending scalewise approach:

Notice: F sharp used to avoid an augmented melodic second.

4. The following examples are less frequent and should be used with extreme caution:

a) This eighth note figure illustrates the use of the infrequent upper auxiliary (see Chapter 23):

b) Extremely rare:

c) Rare. In the "Benedictus" from the Mass *Ut Re Mi Fa Sol La* this figure is found not less than fourteen times. One cannot help feeling that its use in this composition is experimental and not altogether felicitous; the rhythm is spasmodic and not in keeping with the quietness and serenity of a Benedictus. Occasionally a single occurrence of four eighth notes in succession is found, but in all such cases the effect is in good taste.

d) A stepwise descending figure of a dotted half note and a pair of eighth notes followed by an ascending skip of a third is the more frequent of the exceptions under type 4. The skip of a fifth is extremely rare.

The true character of the eighth notes in this style is that of ornament, especially in the suspension formula.

Chapter 22.

Preliminary Exercises in Melody Writing Without Text, Using all Note Values

A CAREFUL perusal of the available material in Chapters 8 and 15 to 21, together with a study of the voice parts in *Examples*, should prepare the student for melody writing using all note values.

Notice the following in addition to the observations already made in Chapter 8:

Half notes may be tied to quarter notes; but quarter notes should not be tied to each other, or to eighth notes, or eighth notes to each other. Repeated quarter notes sometimes occur, apart from the portamento resolution of the suspension; such cases will be described in Chapter 30.

Divide the melody, as done in Chapter 8, in rhythmical groups and indicate the number of beats; also write the melodies, as before, both with and without bar-lines. Each melody will still be considered as the beginning of a composition with the larger note values as initial notes: the dotted half may now be used as an initial note.

All exercises are to be written in $\frac{4}{2}$ time. Write melodies in all modes, ending on a cadence point proper to the mode; sing them, and play them on the instrument of your choice.

The study of melodic line can hardly be overemphasized. While a composition does not depend exclusively on the melodic element, contrapuntal texture demands a skillful handling of melodic material which to a great degree overshadows the harmonic. They are, however, dependent on each other: one furnishes the melodic line, the other the sonority. Both are necessary; but the melodic element is, and always will be, the most important feature in contrapuntal texture.

Chapter 23.

Two-Part Counterpoint Using all Note Values · Quarter Note and Eighth Note Passing Tones · Upper and Lower Auxiliary Notes

---

REVIEW CHAPTER 11.

THE quarter note passing tone is nonessential, or nonharmonic; when the dissonance occurs on the beat the passing tone is said to be accented (being the first of two notes against one), and when off the beat, unaccented (being the second of two notes against one). The half note passing tone, although on the beat, belongs to the latter category.

The accented passing tone occurs on the second or the fourth beats in a downward direction only. It is significant that the first and the third beats were reserved for the suspension dissonance, and that the only other comparatively acute dissonance, i.e., the accented passing tone, occurred on beats two or four in a descending direction like the suspension resolution. This distribution of dissonance emphasizes the importance of the strong beats: the suspension dissonance strongly accentuates the first and the third beats, while the less acute dissonant accented passing tone occurs on the weak beats, i.e., two and four. Conception of the greater rhythm is thus more easily understood, and its relation to secondary rhythm will not seem contradictory.

THE ACCENTED QUARTER NOTE PASSING TONE

The two quarter notes, the first of which is dissonant on the second or the fourth beats, are preceded by either a dotted whole note, a whole note, or a half note; the melodic line is continued either scalewise downwards, or with a stepwise turn, or by skip in the opposite direction. The melodic line:

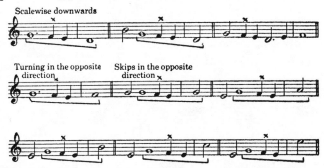

Further examples:

1. The accented passing tone occurring in a scale line:

2. The accented passing tone with a stepwise change in direction:

3. Skips of a third, a fourth, a fifth, a minor sixth, and an octave, in the opposite direction:

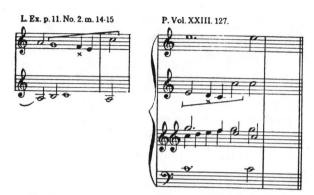

According to Jeppesen,* who uses the term *relatively accented* for this kind of passing tone, the dissonance on the beat should be considered as a grace note to a consonance:

Scalewise descending passages of four quarter notes beginning on strong beats, the first and the second of which are consonant, the third an accented passing tone, occur only with a stepwise change of direction:

See also P. Ex. 24, 35.

This is a standard melodic idiom which is explained by Jeppesen † as a "filled out" Nota Cambiata figure (see Chapter 25):

Although some of these examples are in more than two parts, there can be no objection to the application of the accented passing tone in two-part writing, in the manner shown.

Scalewise descending quarter note passages in which the second and the third notes are dissonant will be illustrated in Chapter 36.

* Jeppesen, *The Style of Palestrina and the Dissonance*, p. 107.
† Jeppesen, *op. cit.*, p. 133.

UNACCENTED QUARTER NOTE PASSING TONES

These passing tones occur on the second half of any beat either ascending or descending.

The quarter notes within a circle are not true passing tones, being consonant. They may be left by skip.

EIGHTH NOTES, PASSING TONES, AND AUXILIARIES

Review Chapter 22.

The location of eighth note pairs on the off beats gives, a priori, the role of unaccented passing tones or of upper or lower auxiliaries.

Eighth notes as passing tones:

Eighth notes with a change of direction:

(1) The first a dissonant passing tone descending to a consonance.
(2) The second a lower auxiliary.
(3) Both consonant.
(4) The first a lower dissonant auxiliary.

In these examples the eighth note pairs are always approached from above; this is the treatment most frequently used in the style.

The following are illustrations of infrequent uses of eighth notes:

P. Ex. 175. 43

A rare upper dissonant auxiliary instead of the usual lower one.

P. Vol. I. 91. 1. 4

The same melodic figure with the first eighth note a dissonant lower auxiliary.

P. Vol. III. 80. 3. 6

Extremely rare; the second eighth note as a consonant upper auxiliary and the high point of the passage.

P. Vol. XXVI. 160. 1. 1-2

Three eighth notes in succession; also extremely rare. No examples have been found in an ascending direction.

P. Ex. 206. 22-23

Four eighth notes in succession are by no means frequent. Their use, previously referred to in Chapter 21, is inadvisable from the point of view of style, unless restricted to a single appearance in a melody.

UPPER AND LOWER AUXILIARY NOTES

Only black note values occur as auxiliaries in $\frac{4}{2}$ time. Auxiliary notes, also called turning notes or neighboring notes, occur on the off beats. They are stepwise, with a stepwise return. They are either consonant or dissonant.

The upper auxiliary most frequently returns to a white note value, but it may also return to a quarter note. It is most frequently consonant; occasionally it occurs as a dissonance, especially in cases where it is first treated as a consonance and then repeated in an imitation as a dissonance because of harmonic considerations. Here, again, the style shows a tendency to abstain from the use of dissonant upper auxiliary notes.

The lower auxiliary is either consonant or dissonant and may be followed by white as well as black note values.

Exercises should now be written using devices illustrated in this chapter. A phrase taken from *Examples* or written by the student should be provided with a counter-subject, below as well as above. Always write an intervallic analysis for each exercise.

Chapter 24.

Ornamented Suspensions · Anticipation · Change of Bass

REVIEW CHAPTER 12.

THE resolution of the suspension is frequently ornamented by a device called portamento. The resolution is anticipated on the off beat and then repeated on the proper beat:

In example (*a*) the 2–3 suspension has a portamento resolution: the resolution is anticipated on the second half of the suspension beat (beat one) and then repeated on the resolution beat (beat two). In the following 2–3 suspension (*b*), the anticipation note on the second half of the third beat is followed by a lower auxiliary which returns to the resolution proper on the fourth beat. Two suspensions immediately following each other are often treated in this manner, especially at a cadence. At (*c*), F is raised to avoid an augmented second.

Other melodic forms of the portamento:

The figure is continued in quarter notes (stepwise) for another beat, invariably followed by an ascending skip:

The same figure, but the skip of the third is abridged by an eighth note passing tone:

The resolution note followed by an eighth note pair in an ascending scale line:

The quarter note on the resolution beat followed by a downward skip of a third and an ascending step:

The same figure with the skip filled out:

The portamento is frequently used as a purely melodic idiom (without suspension). The figure may be preceded by white as well as black note values and is always located on beat one or three. Consonant forms:

THE DISSONANT PORTAMENTO

The dissonant anticipation in the portamento device is used in a descending form only. It is the reverse of the portamento used as a suspension ornament: the initial note is consonant, the anticipation (the second note) is dissonant, and the third note of the figure must be consonant:

Notice that the first note of all these figures is either tied to a previous note or approached stepwise.

Anticipation in an upward direction is rare. It is used in a consonant form only:

CHANGE OF BASS

The bass of the regular suspension usually remains stationary while the suspension dissonance resolves. But the bass may move from the suspension beat to that of the resolution, provided that the resulting interval is a consonance:

a) The bass moves up a second to the resolution beat (see L. Ex. 12, No. 4, 22).

b) The bass moves up a fourth to the resolution beat (see Ex. 14, 27).

c) The bass moves down a third to the resolution beat (see Ex. 49, 47). This is satisfactory only if the suspension is resolved by portamento.

In two parts the change of bass will be confined to the 7–6 suspension only.

Write melodies using the devices illustrated in this chapter; then write counterpoints, above as well as below, to such themes.

Chapter 25.

The Nota Cambiata in Two-Part Texture

REVIEW CHAPTER 16.

THE first and the third notes of the figure must have consonant harmony. The second note (the quarter note) may be treated as a dissonant escape note or as a consonance, while the last note may be a consonance or a passing dissonance. It follows that the first note, the duration of which is one and a half beats, should have a consonance on the first beat as well as on the first half of the second. The initial note of the figure may be placed on any beat in the measure.

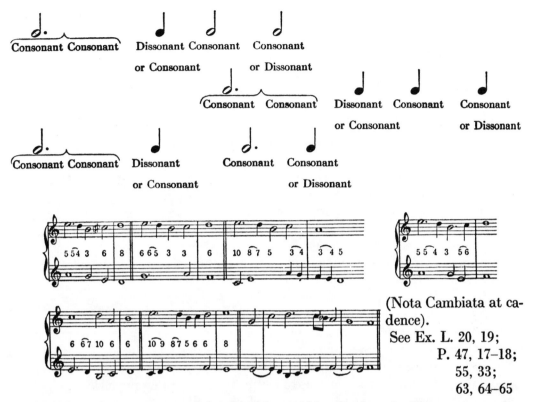

(Nota Cambiata at cadence).
See Ex. L. 20, 19;
P. 47, 17–18;
55, 33;
63, 64–65

This is an incorrect use of the Cambiata evidently thought of as a suspension. The resolution is wrong:

A mirroring, or inversion, of the Cambiata is foreign to the style. But its use in all white note values is correct:

An extension of the Cambiata figure is found in early works by Palestrina *:

The student should now write counterpoints to a phrase containing one or more Cambiatas. A warning against overusing the figure is pertinent, however.

* See Jeppesen, *op. cit.*, p. 196.

Chapter 26.

Cadences and the Hocket

REVIEW CHAPTERS 1 AND 6.

Tₕₑ clausula vera, i.e., the stepwise approach to the cadence point from above and below, will be used exclusively in two-part writing for the present. So far only one-phrase exercises have been assigned; two or more phrases in succession should now be attempted, each ending with a cadence; the first cadence may be any one proper to the mode, but the last one must be on the final of the mode. In order to knit together the different phrases a device called *hocket* frequently is employed.

Hocket (from *hoketus* or *ochetus*, meaning, according to some sources, rhythm, according to others, hiccough) is a name given to a type of thirteenth-century composition in which single notes alternated between the different parts in such a manner that one voice was silent while the other one was singing. Variations of this technique may be found in all styles up to the present. In sixteenth-century polyphonic texture the principle of truncating or interrupting the melody, especially at interior cadences, served the purpose of continuity:

L. Ex. p. 10. No. 1. m. 17-18 Hocket

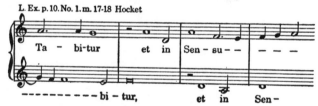

This is an example of the use of a hocket in two parts: the note approaching the cadence point from above becomes the last note of the phrase, a rest taking the place of the cadence point, while the note approaching the cadence point from below (the leading tone) is allowed to proceed to it. While the cadence point is being held, the opposite voice introduces the theme of the next section, or phrase, after the rest, thus producing *dovetailing* or *overlapping*.

The interrupted phrase usually ended with a whole note or a breve on the strong beat; this was the standard procedure except at the final cadence, where the note values were either a breve, a whole note tied to a breve, or a long. Half note phrase endings are relatively infrequent, while endings in still smaller note values do not occur.

Write two- or three-phrase melodies, each ending on a cadence point proper to the mode with accompanying counterpoints above as well as below. Use hockets at interior cadence points.

Chapter 27.

Imitation in Two Parts Using all Note Values

Rᴇᴠɪᴇᴡ:

a) Secondary rhythm and melodic line.
b) Suspensions, ornamentation, and change of resolution intervals.
c) Passing tones.
d) Auxiliary notes.
e) Nota Cambiata.

Exercises should now be written in imitation at various intervals and in different modes. Employ all devices previously illustrated, writing two- or three-phrase exercises, each phrase ending with a cadence proper to the mode, and observing continuity through the use of the hocket. As a general rule use movement against stationary notes.

The following is a brief summary of what may occur on each beat and off beat:

ON BEATS 1 AND 3

Suspension dissonance
Consonance

ON THE OFF BEATS OF 1 AND 3

Consonance
Unaccented passing tones, ascending or descending
Dissonant portamento
Consonant portamento
Nota Cambiata escape note
Lower auxiliary
Upper auxiliary (rare)

ON BEATS 2 OR 4

Consonance
Half note passing tone, ascending or descending
Accented quarter note passing tone, descending only

ON THE OFF BEATS OF 2 OR 4

All devices allowed on off beats of 1 or 3 except consonant and dissonant portamento

An exercise containing common mistakes, prepared by the instructor to be put on the blackboard, is useful in teaching the students to be alert in finding the mistakes in their own exercises. This should be done continuously, especially during the early stages of instruction. The following exercise may serve as a pattern:

(1) Time signature missing.

(2) Rest missing.

(3) A whole note tied to a quarter note (wrong; see Chapter 8). Also, the tie should be in the opposite direction to the stem of the note.

(4) A suspension resolved on the second half of the beat should have been followed by a repetition of the resolution notes on the following beat, i.e., a portamento.

(5) Dissonant ascending quarter note on the beat (wrong).

(6) A suspension dissonance on the wrong beat with a wrong resolution similar to 4.

(7) Melodic tritone skip (wrong).

(8) The Nota Cambiata used as a preparation for a suspension (wrong).

(9) Implied melodic tritone (the Nota Cambiata cannot be used on B for this reason).

(10) Unison on beat (the unison is allowed at the beginning and the end of a phrase and by half notes on beats two or four, when occurring against at least a whole note; by quarter notes on the off beat against at least a half note).

(11) Avoid tying quarter notes to each other (such ties occur very rarely).

(12) Accented ascending quarter note passing tone (wrong).

(13) The fourth on beat two is wrong; it is often analyzed by students, mistakenly, as a lower auxiliary. In this style auxiliaries are found on the off beats only.

(14) When a dotted half and a quarter note occur against two half notes on beats one–two or three–four in two-part writing, both half notes must be consonant with the dotted half. (See Ex. 207, 2, a quite infrequent exception.)

(15) Parallel fifths.

(16) Eighth note pairs must be approached and left by step. (They may, however, in rare instances, be left by skip; see Chapter 23.)

(17) Accented ascending quarter note passing tone (wrong).

(18) Harmonic tritone (wrong).

(19) In two-part writing two successive dissonant passing tones are better avoided (see Chapter 23).

(20) Parallel octaves.

(21) An augmented fifth on beat three (wrong).

Chapter 28.

Double Counterpoint

Two melodies capable of being inverted and of still remaining in correct harmonic agreement with each other are said to be written in double, or invertible, counterpoint. The term double refers to the function of either of the melodies to serve as the upper or the lower part.

The most common intervals of inversion are the octave, the fifteenth, (two octaves), the tenth, and the twelfth.

DOUBLE COUNTERPOINT AT THE OCTAVE

General rules:

1.   The distance between the two voices should not exceed that of an octave in order to avoid crossing of parts. Occasional instances of the distance of an octave being exceeded may be tolerated, however, especially if the melody contains a number of skips. The interval then remains the same as the uninverted one.

   Table of Inversion

2. *Intervals:*   1 2 3 4 5 6 7 8
   Inversions: 8 7 6 5 4 3 2 1

In order to find the correct intervals of inversion the student may consult the tables proper for each kind of inversion, or the interval may be found by subtracting the number of the interval from that of the octave, plus one. For example, if the interval is a sixth, subtract six from nine (8 plus 1); the interval of inversion is a third, and the double counterpoint is at the octave.

On the other hand, to determine which kind of double counterpoint is used in a composition, the number of the first available interval is added to that of the interval of inversion at the corresponding point, minus one. For example, if the interval is a sixth and the inversion shows a third, the added intervals, minus one, show an eight, or double counterpoint at the octave.

3. Since the fifth becomes a fourth in the inversion, it may be used only as a half note or quarter note passing tone on the proper beats.

4. It is preferable not to use the octave or the unison on a strong beat in the texture except at the beginning and at the end of a phrase.

5. The following suspensions may be used: 7–6, 2–3, and 4–3.

6. The contrapuntal texture may be in canonic or free imitation, or it may use two different themes. The interval of imitation may be any of the simple intervals.

7. The clausula vera is the only type of cadence allowed.

8. When inverting the parts, it is often convenient to move each of the two parts a smaller interval than the octave in order to keep the voices within range. Provided that the sum of the two intervals is nine, several combinations are possible. In one of the following examples the upper part (*a*) moved down a fifth, while the lower part (*b*) moved up a fourth.

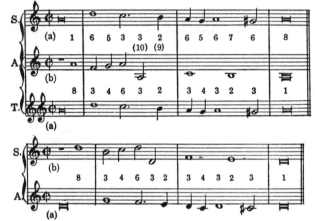

The soprano part is here moved down an octave.

The soprano is moved down a fifth, and the alto moved up a fourth.

9. The common devices of augmentation and diminution, as well as that of mirroring, may be used. Regarding the latter, both Zarlino, in *Institutioni*, and Morley, in *Plaine and Easie Introduction*, present examples of canons in which the original leader may become the follower, and the original follower becomes the leader; the resulting intervals remain the same as in the original. This kind of counterpoint, however, is not capable of being inverted, and suspension dissonances as well as accented quarter note dissonances are excluded. As will be seen from some excerpts from these examples, certain breaches of style are present.* The ascending skip of a quarter note on the beat to another off the beat is very much in evidence because of the mirroring of descending skips; and an ascending quarter note dissonant passing tone is caused by the inversion of a descending accented dissonant quarter note passing tone. In general practice, the ascending quarter note skip to the off beat is rarely found, and the ascending dissonant accented passing tone not at all.

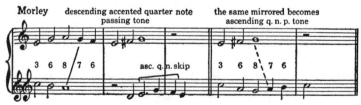

* More freedom is evident in this respect in the style of the English composers of this period.

A short example is furnished by the author, since the afore-mentioned examples are too long to be quoted at length.

The following is an example of double counterpoint at the octave from a Palestrina motet:

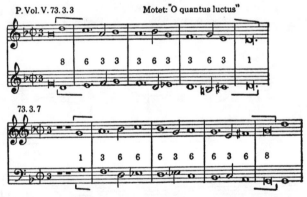

Practice assignments in double counterpoint at the octave:

1. To a theme in whole notes, $\frac{4}{2}$ time, about eight measures in length, write a counterpoint, note against note. End with a clausula vera. No fifths may be used. Several ways of inversion should be practiced, i.e., moving the upper theme down an octave, or the lower theme up an octave, or moving both according to the procedure in section 8. Write in the number of the intervals in the first exercise as well as in the inversion.

2. Write a counterpoint to a theme chosen from *Examples*, for example, page 30, m. 32–36 (end on the first note of m. 36). Use the same procedure as described above. Use all note values as well as allowable dissonances.

3. Write a canon; interrupt the imitation immediately before the cadence. Invert as before.

4. Write several exercises in augmentation, diminution, and mirroring. When inverted in the usual manner, all will be correct.

5. The procedure described in section 9, while not useful in true invertible counterpoint, should be practiced and applied in later exercises.

DOUBLE COUNTERPOINT AT THE FIFTEENTH

Intervals: 1   2   3   4   5   6   7 8 9 10 11 12 13 14 15
Inversions: 15 14 13 12 11 10 9 8 7 6   5   4   3   2   1

The distance between the two parts may exceed that of the octave, but not that of two octaves. For all practical purposes this kind of inversion is the same as that of the octave. The above table is indispensible, however, in order to identify the inversion. The following two examples will prove the point.

In the first example of inversion the tenor has been moved up a fifth and the soprano down an eleventh $(5 + 11 = 16, 16 - 1 = 15)$, and in the second the alto has been moved down a fourth, and the bass up a twelfth $(4 + 12 = 16, 16 - 1 = 15)$. These and other variations of inversion may be found to be more practical, on occasion, than moving one of the parts up or down two octaves.

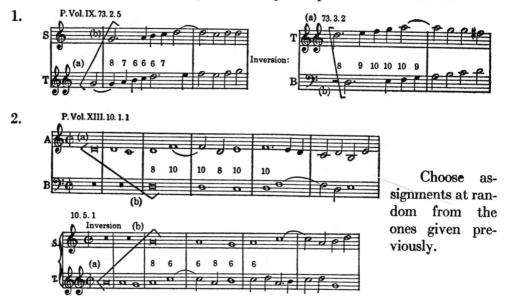

Choose assignments at random from the ones given previously.

DOUBLE COUNTERPOINT AT THE TENTH

Intervals: 1   2 3 4 5 6 7 8 9 10
Inversions: 10 9 8 7 6 5 4 3 2 1

Inversion at the tenth is comparatively infrequent. A rare example by Palestrina will be found in the section Double Counterpoint at the Twelfth.

The following rules must be observed:

1. Motion of consecutive consonant intervals is forbidden (parallel thirds become parallel octaves, and parallel sixths become parallel fifths).

Care must be exercised in the approach to thirds and sixths because of the danger of exposed octaves and fifths in the inversion. Oblique or contrary motion is mandatory in such cases; the sixth, however, may be approached by skip in the upper voice and step in the lower, in the same direction.

2. The only suspension possible is the 2–3 (preferably in more than two-part writing).

3. See rule 8 in the section Double Counterpoint at the Octave regarding inversion.

4. In order to produce a satisfactory cadence, the texture may revert to free counterpoint near the cadence point.

5. The distance between the two parts may not exceed that of a tenth.

Example in note against note:

Example using all note values:

Assignment: Write exercises similar to the ones above, with the addition of numbers 3 and 4 given in the section Double Counterpoint at the Octave.

DOUBLE COUNTERPOINT AT THE TWELFTH

Intervals: 1 2 3 4 5 6 7 8 9 10 11 12
Inversions: 12 11 10 9 8 7 6 5 4 3 2 1

This species is one of the most useful in sixteenth-century practice.

Rules:

1. The distance between the two parts may not exceed that of a twelfth.

2. Because of the width of the inversion it is often divided between the parts, i.e., the upper part may be moved down a fifth or an octave, and the lower part moved up an octave or a fifth $(5 + 8 = 13); (13 - 1 = 12)$. See examples 1 and 4 below.

3. The following suspensions are possible: 2–3, which becomes 4–3, and 4–3, which becomes 2–3. The 7–6 may be used if the sixth continues down by step, thereby becoming a dissonant descending half note or an accented descending quarter note passing tone in the inversion. See examples 2 and 3 below.

4. The cadence is free.

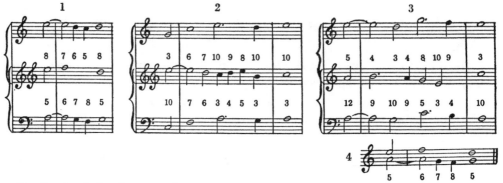

Study the following exercises:

In the following example from Palestrina (a) 1 is found inverted at the twelfth at (a) 2, while (b) 1 is inverted at the tenth at (b) 2:

Notice the brevity of the inversions: they are rarely continued beyond a measure or two. The freedom of contrapuntal texture is in evidence always.

Assignments: 1, 2, 3, and 4, given in the section Double Counterpoint at the Octave.

Chapter 29+

Triple Time

Vᴀʀɪᴏᴜs types of triple time signatures are used in the style. In the Gloria and the Credo, and in a number of other compositions, duple time is sometimes interrupted by short sections of triple time in which white note values are used exclusively, or white notes and occasional pairs of quarter notes. This kind of triple time indicates a tempo faster than the previous duple time, the relation being expressed in the proportional sign (the time signature). The note values, in such cases, become either 3 or $1\frac{1}{2}$ times faster.

There are, however, compositions in triple time that use all note values which indicate a moderate tempo, at any rate not so fast as the "tripla" mentioned previously. The latter is the kind of triple time which will be considered in this chapter (see Ex. 226).

For practical purposes the half note, the time unit of duple time, will be the time unit here also. The time signature will be $\frac{6}{2}$.

All rules are to be applied in the same manner as in $\frac{4}{2}$. A few observations are pertinent.

SUSPENSIONS

Their location is, as before, on the odd beats, and the preparation and resolution on the even beats:

	Preparation	Suspension	Resolution		Preparation	Suspension	Resolution
Beats:	6	1	2	3	4	5	6

Preparation Suspension Resolution

CADENCES

In interior cadences the final cadence chord should fall on beats one, three, or five. The final cadence at the end of a composition should, as a rule, fall on beat one.

SECONDARY RHYTHM

Continued effort in this respect is paramount. Special attention should be paid to the meter of three whole notes against two dotted whole notes:

PASSING TONES

Ascending and descending half note passing tones occur on even beats as the second of two half notes against at least a whole note; descending accented quarter note passing tones on even beats as the first of two quarter notes against at least a half note, and unaccented passing tones on the off beat of any beat, both ascending and descending.

The following example in $\frac{6}{2}$ time employs two themes which are inverted, in the second phrase, in double counterpoint at the twelfth. The inversion is interrupted before the cadence:

Assignment:

1. Write a number of melodies in triple time using all note values. As usual, write in various modes, ending with a cadence point proper to the mode.

2. Write counterpoints to these melodies, employing the contrapuntal devices in use up to this point.

3. Write short exercises in imitation and also exercises capable of inversion in the octave, the tenth, and the twelfth.

Chapter 30.

The Setting of Texts · Latin Pronunciation

THE agogic accents which indicate the beginning of rhythmical groups should be made to coincide with the metrical accents of the words. The following excerpt from Ex. 45, 22–25, illustrates the point:

Dó --- mi-nus Dé - us Sá --------ba-oth

Since it is customary to begin a composition with long note values (none smaller than a dotted half), it will be necessary also to place the first accent on anacrustic syllables (from *anacrusis*, meaning one or several unstressed syllables prefixed to a word) when they are the initial word of a text. Such syllables are treated as up-beats during the texture, however, and generally fall on even (weak) beats, but there is no objection to placing the accent (long note) on them also during the texture (see Ex. 164, 11–12 and 18–19).

P.Ex.164.1   P.Ex.164.7-8

Ho ---- sán ---na   Ho - śan-na in

The rules for the setting of texts, generally followed by the composers of the sixteenth century, were as follows:

1. Only white note values may carry a syllable.

2. No syllable change was allowed after a quarter note or eighth note pairs; thus a quarter note passage had to reach a white note before changing:

P. Ex. 25. 72-74

e ----------------- lei - son

3. Words with accentuation, such as Kyrie, Domine, and Spiritu, may change syllable after a quarter note, if it is preceded by a dotted half note and followed by a white note value; Kyrie may also be a two syllable word (see example).

P.188.82.84   P.22.1-2   P.22.11-12

Ký-ri-e   e -lei -- son   Ký - ri - e e-lei-   Ký-rie e-lei ------

4. No eighth notes may carry a syllable.

5. The first note of a quarter note passage may carry a syllable; also, an interior phrase may begin with a quarter note passage of not less than four notes.

6. Should the final note of a section or a movement be preceded by a quarter note, a change of syllable may be permitted on the final note. (Rare)

7. In imitation the arrangement of syllable must be exactly the same in all voices as that of the first appearance of the theme.

8. Every repeated note which has not the character of ornamentation demands a new syllable. Thus the repeated quarter notes in the following example must each have a syllable; such examples and others with exceptional text settings are mostly found in Palestrina's Motets.

et   dul - ci - a   po - ma   de   lig - no   de - cer - pit

9. At the end of a composition (or a section) the last syllable, although not a metrical accent, will fall on beat one or three.

Exceptions to these rules may be found, but the student should apply the general usage in his exercises. They are adequate for the purpose for which they were formulated.

The setting of texts should begin with single melodic lines. Do not write the melody first and then try to fit the words to it. Begin with the first word, projecting the melody in the desired direction and placing the accents properly as the setting proceeds. Use short sentences in the beginning, such as "Kyrie eleison," or "Hosanna in excelsis." *Examples* offers a great variety of patterns for study. Make the melody rhythmically interesting.

Besides Latin, English texts should be used. The translations found in the back of *Examples* will serve for the purpose, or other Bible texts. Apply the same rules as for Latin.

LATIN PRONUNCIATION

The modified or double vowel sounds of English have no counterpart in Latin; in the latter the vowels have one uniform sound.

The following is an approximate comparison between the vowel sounds in Latin and English.

> A as in far
> E as in met (short *e*), and as in they (long *e*)
> I as in marine
> O as in chord
> U as in rule
> Y as the Latin I

Two or three consecutive vowels are pronounced separately:

> IEI   di-e-i
> AIE   a-i-e-bat
> IE   faci-e, hodi-e
> II   labi-is

EA	fate-ature
EI	e-is, me-i
EO	e-orum
EU	De-us
IO	redempti-o
OU	co-untuntur
OI	co-inquinati
UI	potu-istis
UU	su-um

AE and OE pronounced as one vowel, the Latin E.

AU, EU, AY have emphasis on the first vowel, the second belonging, more or less, to the next syllable. If these double vowels are set to a passage of several notes, the passage should be sung on the first vowel leaving the last note for the second vowel (see Ex. 168, 4–6, alto).

Q, and NG, followed by U and another vowel have the emphasis on the second vowel and form one syllable; qui, quoniam.

Cui (cu-i) is distinct from qui.

Consonants:

C before e, i, y, ae, and oe sounds like ch in child. Acete — achete, amici — ameeche, caelestis — chelestis, coeli — chelie.

CC followed by similar vowels: acceperant — acheperant.

SC followed by similar vowels: sounds like sh in she; suscipe — soosheepe.

C before a, o, u, has the sound of k as in call; ch sounds like k before all letters.

G before e, i, y, ae, and oe is like g in gem; celligent. Otherwise it is pronounced as in English.

GN is pronounced as ny in canyon; regna — renya.

H is mute except in mihi (meekee) and nihil (neekeel) and compounds of nihil.

J is like y in Yale: je junierum — yeyooneeoroom; alleluja or alleluia — alle-looya.

R should be pronounced with a rolling sound.

S is always pronounced as in sit.

TI followed by a vowel and preceded by any letter except S, T, or X is pronounced tsi (tsee): sapientia — sahpee-entseea.

TH always has the t sound of English.

X is pronounced as in English. Some combinations with other consonants: XC before e or i — ksh: excelsis — ekshelsees. In all other cases ksk: exclama-verunt.

The remaining consonants are pronounced as in English. Double consonants must both be enunciated: bello (bel-lo).

Chapter 31.

Analysis of Two-Part Compositions • Two-Part Counterpoint with Text

BEFORE attempting two-part counterpoint with text a thorough analysis should be made of the two-part Cantiones by Lassus, in *Examples*.

1. Harmonic analysis by interval: Indicate all intervals by number between the staffs. In at least three cantiones a tabulation of the intervals should be made (how many of each) as an index of the prevalence of each.

2. Analyze the imitations, beat for beat; notice changes in the imitation interval. Also notice whether the theme and its imitation agree as regards the text.

3. Find all suspensions and passing tones.

4. State the mode; find all cadences and observe whether they are proper to the mode. (No. 3, which ends in the Dorian mode, begins in the Phrygian mode and continues in this mode for fifteen measures, ending the section on a Phrygian cadence.)

5. Indicate, by slurs or by accent marks, the secondary rhythm groups in several cantiones.

6. Notice how phrases begin and end in regard to note values and rests.

7. Notice the procedure in dovetailing cadences and in the use of the hocket.

8. For those not familiar with Latin there are translations at the end of *Examples*.

TWO-PART COUNTERPOINT WITH TEXT

Follow the procedure described in the previous chapter in regard to the setting of texts. After having chosen the text, the mode, and the interval of imitation, the writing will proceed along lines already familiar to the student. The "Benedictus" found on page 20 in *Examples* is a good model. Longer texts should follow, such as those of the Cantiones or the shorter movements of the Mass, in Latin or in English.

The form is sectional, akin to *through composed*. A certain part of the text, a sentence, or a single word, should be chosen for each section and should arrive at a cadence proper to the mode, maintaining continuity with the next section unless the text demands an outright stop, such as at a period, colon, or semicolon. The cadence at the end should be that of the final of the mode.

Most cadences are preceded by a suspension to the leading tone (*not* to the cadence point). At times a word, or several words, are set to a short melodic phrase interrupted by a rest; in such cases a cadence is not necessary.

The student should become familiar with the Cantiones not only through analysis, but also through singing them; this applies to his own exercises as well.

PART THREE

Counterpoint
in Three Parts

Chapter 32.

Counterpoint in Three Parts · Harmonic Material · Cadences

T HE vertical aspect of two-part counterpoint dealt with single intervals. With the addition of a third part the vertical structure becomes more complex; chord progression, or chordal background, comes into being. It would be a mistake to proceed from a preconceived harmony, letting passing tones and other devices *make* counterpoint in the parts. The melodic element should be predominant. According to the direction in which the melody is *projected* certain sonorities, or harmonies, will result. Even in compositions which are classed as homophonic the voice leading is distinctly melodic.

The basic harmonic intervals are the same as in two parts, i.e., consonances. In three parts two consonant intervals are combined. The following basic chord structures are the result of such combinations:

Notice that the analysis is made from the lowest note (in pitch) to each of the notes above. Such analysis is called two-part horizontal, and will be employed throughout in all compositions. It is said that the upper parts *agree* with the lowest (in pitch) part. The upper two parts may now form a perfect, an augmented, or a diminished fourth or fifth.

The available material in the untransposed modes follows:

Major and minor triads are used in root positions and first inversions; diminished and augmented triads may be used in first inversions only. The ⁶₅ chord will be described in Chapters 38–43. Its dissonant character classes it almost exclusively among the suspensions.

In looking over this material, it will be noticed that a triad has been placed on each of the white notes of the keyboard; in addition, the triads modified by *musica ficta,* i.e., the accidentals F sharp, C sharp, G sharp, and B flat are used. Two sharps, or a sharp and a flat, in the same chord are forbidden.

The major and the minor triads occur with greatest frequency; the diminished triads are less frequent and the augmented triads are quite rare. The B minor triad occurs with the utmost rarity. The bulk of the texture thus is consonant; the diminished triads mostly have cadential implications, and the augmented triads occur where textual expression * demands their use. The B minor triad is quite alien to the key feeling of the modes.

Good sonority demands the presence of all notes in the triad. Any note, however, may be doubled except one which has a sharp and E or B as the leading tone in a cadence. Great care must be observed not to thin the texture in places which obviously demand full sonority, such as accents or climaxes. Close position is preferable, but comparatively wide spacing sometimes is inevitable; such spacing is very effective at times, but it should be used sparingly, always with a return to close position.

CADENCES

1. To the clausula vera type of cadence a third part is added which, when in the lowest part, results in what was later called the authentic cadence. The initial cadence chord, a complete triad, progresses to a triple final or a double final and a third; the bass, or the lowest part, moves up a fourth or down a fifth (see types *a, b, c, d*).

The complete diminished triad in the first inversion as an initial cadence chord, also the clausula vera type, progresses to a double final and a fifth or a fourth (see types *e* and *f*). This is sometimes called the leading tone cadence.

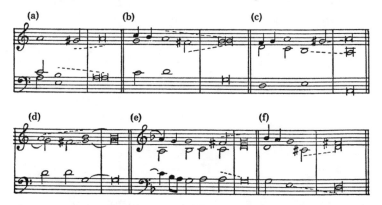

2. Another cadence type of great frequency, later called the plagal cadence, is based on a root movement of a fifth up or a fourth down. The complete initial cadence chord progresses to a double final and a fifth, type *a*, or the initial chord, with doubled root and a third, to a complete triad, type *b*.

---

* On such words as death, grief, tears, and torment, the augmented triad was the standard chord of expression in the sixteenth century in both ecclesiastical and secular music.

See Ex. 24, 60–61.
See Ex. 26, 92–93.

3. The Phrygian cadence.

This cadence is a clausula vera type. The initial chord (complete) in the first inversion moves to a double final and a major third or, rarely, a minor third. The final may be on E as well as on A: D minor to E major, and G minor to A major. See types *a* and *b* and Ex. 22, 9–10; 24, 33; 35, 126–27; 46, 43–44; 60, 88–89.

4. The deceptive (interrupted) cadence.

Near the end of a phrase the initial cadence chord of an intended authentic cadence sometimes changes its direction. The effect is that of interruption or deception. In the most commonly used progressions the bass proceeds stepwise up, the second (deceptive) chord occurring in root position or in the first inversion; or the bass goes down stepwise, the second chord a triad in root position (see types *a, b, c, d*). *C* and *d* might also be classed together, since the root of the second chord, in both cases, is a second lower than that of the initial chord. See Ex. 22, 13; 23, 26–27; 24, 43–44; 24, 58–59; 52, 30; 64, 72–73; 119, 32–33; 195, 59–60.

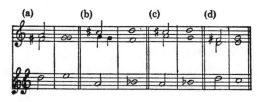

SUMMARY

1. In all concluding cadences the two chords are in root position except the Phrygian, in which the initial chord is in the first inversion and the final in root position. In the final chord, the third, if present, is always major in all concluding cadences (with extremely few exceptions).

2. The clausula vera is the basis for all cadences here enumerated except the plagal.

3. The initial chord of the plagal cadence is minor in the Dorian, Phrygian, and Aeolian modes, major in the Ionian, Lydian, and Mixolydian.

4. The initial chord of the leading tone cadence is diminished and in the first inversion.

5. Interior cadences may be of any type; in light cadences either of the two chords may be in the first inversion. See Ex. 23, 15–16; 23, 19–20; 27, 11–12.

Concluding and Interior Cadences	*Interior Cadences Only*
G–D	A–d
g–D	E–a
A–D	g–a
d–E	
a–E	*All Leading Tone Cadences*
C–F	
B flat–F	
D–G	
C–G	
E–A	
d–A	
g–A	
F–B flat	
E flat–B flat (transposed modes)	
G–C	
F–C	

Chapter 33.

Note Against Note

THE aim of this chapter is to combine acceptable melodic lines with an interesting harmonic background.

1. The choice of voices may vary a great deal; any combination is possible provided that the range of each voice is in a favorable register and that the sonority is satisfactory. Only the lowest voice may, occasionally, exceed the distance of an octave to the next voice above. The upper voices should not be more than an octave apart:

Beginning and cadence only

2. For the present, repeated notes should be avoided or at least limited to two in succession.

3. *Musica ficta* may be used in the texture (sparingly), and always in the cadences.

4. Parallel fifths and octaves are forbidden. The former may occasionally be avoided by crossing, or by use of portamento in one of the parts (Ex. 24, 32).

5. Hidden or exposed fifths and octaves are permitted between any parts if one of the parts moves stepwise and the other by skip:

Skips in both voices in the same direction to a fifth or an octave should be avoided, but may occur in four parts or more (Ex. 119, 24, 137, 38).

6. Unisons are allowed between any two parts. They should be approached and left by contrary or oblique motion.

7. All rules regarding the conduct of the melodic line remain in force.

8. It is preferable to indicate the mode by beginning on the final (tonic) or the dominant.

9. Any note in a chord may be doubled except the leading tone (the note going to the cadence point).

10. Progressions in which all voices skip in the same direction are inadvisable; at least one voice should proceed by step, in the same direction, or in contrary motion.

11. The leading tone usually goes into the cadence point, but may occasionally skip down a third (in four or more parts). See Ex. 74, 22; 113, 27. It may be approached by the skip of a third from above or below.

CHORD PROGRESSIONS

The urgency of dissonance determined the direction of a progression. Thus the suspension, being a dissonance, demanded a resolution, while major and minor triads, being consonances, were free in their movements. The greater part of the harmonic material consisted of major and minor triads; the freedom of their use and the absence of modulation in the modern sense set the harmonic element of the sixteenth-century ecclesiastical style, and, to a lesser degree, the secular style, apart from that of later styles.

The melodic element, to a great degree stepwise, also contributed to the character of harmonic progression; adjacent chords were frequent. It is important to note that up or down, stepwise, chord root progressions were approximately thirty per cent more numerous than those of a third, up or down. Also, roots up a third (infrequent in later styles), occur more than thirty per cent of the total of roots up or down a third. The order of frequency of root movements follows:

1. A fourth up (or a fifth down)
2. A fifth up (or a fourth down)
3. A second up
4. A second down
5. A third down
6. A third up.

This tabulation is based on one small collection (the first edition of *Examples of Gregorian Chant and Works by Orlandus Lassus and Giovanni Pierluigi Palestrina*, the analysis including Palestrina only, since Lassus is represented by two-part compositions). In view of the homogeneity of the ecclesiastical style as a whole, this tabulation may be assumed to be valid for this period at least. Single compositions vary in some degree, which the (approximate) harmonic index of the Offertory *Exaltabo Te* (Ex. 177) shows:

Fifth up	23	per cent
Fourth up	21	" "
Third up	8	" "
Third down	15	" "
Second up	19	" "
Second down	14	" "

It is hardly necessary to go further into statistics. Suffice it to say that the most prevalent major and minor triads are those on the first, fourth, and fifth degree (not necessarily in that order).

The use of B flat gives additional color to the harmonic texture; it is found in all modes, without exception. The student should analyze each case closely.

Assignment: Write exercises in three parts, note against note (one voice part to each staff) patterned on the following examples:

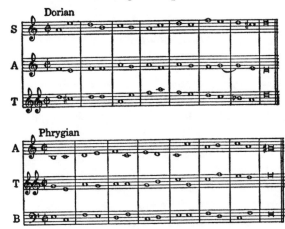

Chapter 34.

Half Note Passing Tones

Use all white note values except the dotted half. Previous rules regarding half note passing tones remain in force (see Chapter 10).

Additional rules:

1. A half note passing tone against a harmony skip in white notes must be consonant with the note which skips:

2. Double half note passing tones, in parallel thirds and sixths only, may be used in similar motion:

3. Double half note passing tones in contrary motion may be unisons, thirds, sixths, or octaves:

See the end of Chapter 4, where the Amen from the Credo from the *Pope Marcellus* Mass contains numerous examples of single, double, and triple half note passing tones. See also Ex. 24, 47; 100, 85–86.

Assignment: Write exercises patterned on the following examples:

Chapter 35.

Suspensions

REVIEW CHAPTERS 11 AND 24.

THE 7–6 SUSPENSION IN ITS REGULAR FORM.

THE addition of a third part results in the figuring: (*a*) $\frac{7}{3}$, (*b*) $\frac{7}{5}$, (*c*) $\frac{8}{7}$. The consonances available for the added part thus are the third, the fifth, and the octave. Of these, the fifth, if remaining during the resolution, will cause a dissonance with it. General practice makes it evident that this dissonance was avoided, the fifth moving down to the third or moving up into the resolution. As will be seen later, the fifth occasionally remained, however, in four or more parts (see Ex. 210, 8).

The resolution chord is always a first inversion of a triad (see Ex. 27, 6; 28, 17; 144, 15; 166, 22; 167, 39; 168, 5).

In general, the note of the resolution should not be present, in another voice, on the beat of the suspension dissonance. While there are some exceptions, especially in many-voiced compositions, there is little doubt that the logical formula of the suspension is disturbed thereby (see Ex. 203, 72).

Irregular treatment of the 7–6 suspension.

a) The bass moves up a second to the resolution beat; the resolution chord is a triad in root position (see Ex. 207, 40; 197, 56).

b) The bass moves up a fourth or down a fifth to the resolution beat; the resolution chord is a triad in root position (see Ex. 203, 73).

c) The bass moves down a third to the resolution beat. The resolution chord may be triad in root position or a first inversion (Ex. 49, 63). For use in four or more parts, see Ex. 73, 10, and 40; 161, 46; 175, 54; 203, 85.

THE 2–3 SUSPENSION

The 2–3 suspension may be considered as an inversion of the 7–6 suspension. The suspension melody is now in the lower voice. The addition of a third voice results in the figuring (*a*) and (*b*) $\frac{4}{2}$, (*c*) $\frac{5}{2}$, (*d*) $\frac{6}{2}$, and (rarely) (*e*) $\frac{3}{2}$.

Since the interval of a second (or a ninth) must be present, the added interval should belong to the chord of the resolution and may or may not be dissonant with the suspended note. It may also be consonant with the suspended note, in which case it is dissonant with the resolution chord and has to move to a consonant member of the resolution chord.

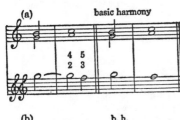

a) Both the fourth and the second are dissonant with the suspended note and remain as members of the resolution chord (see Ex. 158, 4).

b) The same as above, but the fourth moves up stepwise, resulting in a first inversion of a triad (see Ex. 79, 76).

c) The fifth is consonant and the second is dissonant with the suspended note; both remain as members of the resolution chord (see Ex. 22, 11).

P. Ex. 72. 20.

d) The sixth is consonant and the second is dissonant with the suspended note; the sixth being dissonant with the resolution chord must move to a chord note, the second remaining as a member of the resolution chord (see Ex. 164, 3).

e) The second becomes the member of the resolution chord; the third is consonant with the suspended note, and has to move to a note in the resolution chord, either down or up (see Ex. 209, 30; 202, 55).

The bass may sometimes be changed through crossing of parts. The examples quoted in this chapter and later may serve as a guide as to how far one may go in this direction.

Two suspensions, the 4–5 and the 7–8, remain to be discussed. It is doubtful that they were considered as legitimate suspension dissonances at any time in the sixteenth century; at least their rarity mitigates against such a supposition. It is interesting to note that both of these "suspensions" almost invariably are found as complementary notes in the 2–3 suspension formula, and hardly ever alone (see Ex. 118, 35).

Jeppesen's analysis * of the examples quoted is as follows:

(*a*) a 4–5 suspension, the fifth perfect; (*b*) and (*c*) a 4–5 suspension, the fifth diminished.

If vertical analysis establishes the lowest note (in pitch) as the basis for figuring, it is hard to understand the analysis thus presented. Analysis from the bass up shows at *a:* a 2–3 suspension with the resolution present in another voice; at *b:* a 7–6 suspension; at *c:* a 2–3 suspension with a rare diminished fifth in the resolution chord. (The 7–8 will be found in the list of double suspensions later in this chapter.)

* Jeppesen, *op. cit*, pp. 225–226.

The bass of the suspension beat occasionally moves in quarter note values. It must, however, arrive at a consonance on the resolution beat, through a lower auxiliary, or by an ascending or descending unaccented passing tone (see Ex. 68, 9).

P. Vol. X. 65.5. 2-3

THE 4–3 SUSPENSION

The addition of a third part results in the figuring (*a*) and (*b*) $\frac{5}{4}$, (*c*) and (*d*) $\frac{6}{4}$, and (*e*) $\frac{8}{4}$.

a) The fifth remains; the resolution chord is a triad (see Ex. 22, 6).

b) The octave moves to the sixth; the resolution chord is a first inversion (see Ex. 96, 72).

c) The sixth moves to the fifth; the resolution chord is a triad (see Ex. 90, 6).

d) The sixth remains; the resolution chord is a first inversion (see Ex. 71, 4).

e) The octave remains; the resolution chord is a triad (see Ex. 71, 35).

f) The fourth is augmented (see Ex. 46, 6).

Change of bass.

The bass moves down a third to the resolution chord (see Ex. 94, 34).

CHANGE OF BASS THROUGH CROSSING OF PARTS

The bass note under the suspended note skips up a fifth (see Ex. 153, 81) or an octave (see Ex. 25, 71) to the third, or the sixth above the resolution note, which now becomes bass:

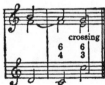

Study the following examples of 4–3 suspensions with the resolution present: Ex. 50, 72; 62, 38; 92, 37; 113, 26; 211, 12.

THE 9–8 SUSPENSION

This suspension is relatively infrequent. In three parts the only forms which occur are the $\frac{9}{3}$ and the $\frac{9}{6}$ (see Ex. 22, 7; 24, 54).

CHANGE OF BASS

The following examples have been found:

In four parts: The bass skipping a third down to the resolution beat: 152, 68. The same effect through the addition of a bass note (Ex. 46, 38).

The bass skipping up a third to the resolution beat: Ex. 62, 30; 160, 29.

In three parts: The bass skipping down a fifth to the resolution beat:

P. Vol. XI. 90. 1. 3-5

 By crossing of parts: Ex. 45, 33; the effect is that of skipping down a third.

THE 2–1 SUSPENSION

The 2–1 suspension (the 9–8 telescoped, as it were), occurs with sufficient frequency to merit attention. It occurs with the figuring $\frac{3}{2}$ and $\frac{5}{2}$.

P. Ex. 24. 43.   P. Ex. 167. 27.

See Ex. 30, 48; 46, 37; 49, 51; 50, 66; 56, 4; 112, 5; 119, 27; 197, 47; 203, 64.

Although not very frequent, a series of successive suspensions is quite effective:

P. Ex. 206. 4-7.

DOUBLE SUSPENSIONS

The following double suspensions occur with relative frequency: $^{7-6}_{4-3}$, $^{9-8}_{4-3}$, and $^{7-8}_{2-3}$ (extremely rare).

Parallel fifths between the notes of resolution will occur in the $^{7-6}_{4-3}$ double suspension, if the fourth is placed above the seventh. They are avoided by resolving the seventh (see Ex. 56, 9) or the fourth (see Ex. 87 , 5) by portamento.

The double suspensions occur mostly in four or more parts. Quite often the resolution of one of the suspensions is present in another part. As for their use in three parts, the $^{9-8}_{4-3}$ seems to be more prevalent (see Ex. 52, 29), although there seems to be no valid reason for not using the $^{7-6}_{4-3}$ in three parts.

The $^{7-8}_{2-3}$ (see Ex. 207, 35) is exceedingly rare in the style (see the reference to the 7–8 suspension earlier in this chapter). It might be analyzed as a 2–3 suspension with the resolution present.

Further analysis of voice leading should be made by the student in *Examples*.

Assignments:

1. Write eight-measure themes containing suspension melodies.

2. Use the themes alternately as the upper, middle, or lower part, adding the two other parts. Use suspensions in all their forms. End with a cadence proper to the mode.

Chapter 36.

Use of Quarter Notes, Eighth Notes, Portamento, Anticipation, and Auxiliary Notes

THE rules given in Chapter 23 are valid for three parts and should be reviewed thoroughly. Since each upper part must agree with the lower part, there are in reality several sets of two parts in compositions for three parts or more.

A recapitulation of intervallic relationships between parts, valid for three or more parts, is desirable at this point:

1. Consonant agreement between the lower part and each of the upper parts, each part moving simultaneously from one sonority to another (note against note),

is known as chord progression or homophony. It remains to be seen to what degree the two upper parts agree with each other.

The two upper parts may be consonant with each other as well as with the lower part; it is interesting to note that from about 1460 to 1520 a distinctive trend in this direction may be found.* But in the sixteenth century dissonances were used freely between the upper parts, provided that they agreed with the lower part. These dissonances were: major and minor seconds, perfect, diminished, and augmented fourths, augmented and diminished fifths, major and minor sevenths. Of these only the fourths and the fifths will be considered in this section. They occur between the upper parts in inversions of all the triads:

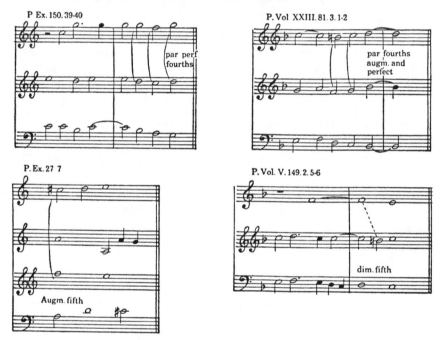

See also Ex. 85, 190–191.

2. Shorter note values in the upper parts moving against stationary notes in the lower part are either passing tones, portamentos, anticipations, or auxiliary notes, or they are consonances, in which case they have freedom of movement. The principle is briefly this: A consonance with the lower part may be approached and left by step or skip; a dissonance, by step only. The Nota Cambiata is an exception (see the examples quoted in Chapter 25).

Motion in similar note values between the upper parts against a stationary lower part is usually consonant; the upper parts move in parallel thirds or sixths, occasionally parallel fourths, and dissimilar consonances. But dissonances occur occasionally, if infrequently, especially in the $\frac{6}{5}$ (see Chapters 38 to 43).

---

* See the article in the *Musical Quarterly* (January, 1945, Vol. XXXI, No. I) on "Non-Quartal Harmony in the Renaissance" by Charles Warren Fox.

a) In a scalewise descending passage of four quarter notes beginning on a strong beat, an unaccented quarter note passing tone may be followed by an accented quarter note passing tone, provided the passage changes direction by step (see Chapter 23).

b) Similar note values descending in parallel thirds. Being consonant on the beats, they may change direction freely, or continue the scalewise motion, ascending or descending.

c) Consonant portamento.

P. Vol. XXIII. 105.3. 1·2

d) A scalewise descending passage of four quarter notes, the first and the second notes consonant, the third an accented quarter note passing tone. The passage changes direction by step.

P. Ex. 24. 34·35 (d)

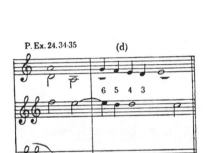

e) Here a dissonance is produced by an unaccented passing tone moving against a Nota Cambiata (see also Ex. 78, 60).

P. Ex. 78. 47-48 (e)

3. When the upper parts move in dissimilar note values, dissonant clashes may occur between the upper parts as well as between the lower and the moving parts. The examples quoted show parallel seconds, fourths, and sevenths. One of the upper parts must be a descending quarter note passage of four notes returning upwards by step.

P. Ex. 24. 38-39 (a)

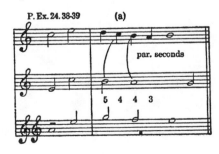

a) Parallel seconds between the upper parts, parallel fourths between the lower and the upper part.

P. Vol. V. 42. 4. **7**
43. 1. 1-2

par. seconds

5 4 4 3

The same with different approach.

P. V. 81. 1. 3-4   (b)

par. sevenths

8 7 6 5

b) Parallel sevenths between the upper parts; consonances on the beats between the lower and the middle part.

4. Should the lower part be moving in shorter note values against stationary notes in one or all of the upper voices, one of the upper parts, or a note in one of the upper parts, assumes the former role of the lower part (in reverse, as it were) for the duration of the moving notes.

P. V. 65. 3. 2-3

10   8   5
3 1 3 1 3 3 3 3   3

Consonances on the beats, followed by unaccented quarter note passing tones (see also P. Ex. 78, 46).

P. Vol. XXIII. 116. 2. 2-3

lower auxiliary
↓ 6 6 7 8

P. Vol. XV. 88. 3. 4

3 6 7 8

An accented quarter note passing tone in the lower part.

See also P. Ex. 76, 16; 81, 123 (double acc. p. t.). See section 5.

P. V. 58. 3. 2-3

6 7 7 8 par. sevenths

3 4 4 5

par. fourths

Parallel sevenths between the lower and the upper parts; parallel fourths between the lower and the middle parts.

Le Huerter:
Mass: "Osculetur Me" Sanctus: p. 187. m. 70

6
5

6 7 7 8

Parallel sevenths between the lower and the middle parts.

5. Occasionally one of upper parts disagrees with the lower part while agreeing with the other:

P. Ex. 136. 13

In the example quoted the upper part agrees with both the lower and the middle parts, but the lower part disagrees with the middle part in that the dissonance of a fourth appears on the second beat. The term *double analysis* is in order for similar cases.

6. Harmony skips in one part against dissonant passing tones in another part may occur between accented quarter note passing tones and harmony skips in white note values:

P. Ex. 50. 68-69
See Ex. 94. 46

(a)

a) Harmony skip in half notes; the dissonance occurs on the beat (see Ex. 94, 46).

P. Ex. 94. 40

b) Between unaccented quarter note passing tones and harmony skips in quarter notes; the dissonance occurs on the half beat (see Ex. 156, 5; 159, 20; 185, 9; 188, 83; 209, 45).

LOWER AND UPPER AUXILIARIES.
REVIEW CHAPTER 24.

As stated previously, similar note values usually move together consonantly, but may be either consonant or dissonant with the lower part.

In the following examples the lower auxiliary moves dissonantly against another upper part:

Against a portamento, causing parallel seconds

Against an unaccented passing tone, causing parallel fourths

P. Ex. 164. 4-5

P. Ex. 192. 90

Double lower auxiliaries usually occur as parallel thirds (see Ex. 58, 56; 70, 8) and (rarely) as parallel fourths (see Ex. 60, 88; 97, 30).

Upper auxiliaries are much less frequent. An interesting example follows:

P. Vol. XXIII. 97. 3. 8

See further Ex. 24, 37; 71, 3; 83, 152; 84, 173 and 176; 90, 11, 15, 17, and 19; 139, 72.

PORTAMENTO · ANTICIPATION

Portamento, both as ornamentation of the resolution of the suspension and as an independent, purely melodic figure, usually agrees consonantly with similar moving note values in another part (see Ex. 33, 100; 46, 6).

Some exceptional examples of dissonance between the moving parts follow:

Against an unaccented passing tone causing the dissonance of a fourth

Also against an unaccented passing tone causing a diminished fifth

P. Ex. 83. 161

P. Vol. XXIII. 100. 1. 2-3

P. Ex. 74. 32-33

A dissonant (with the lower part) portamento against an unaccented passing tone.

Double portamento always agrees consonantly; they are usually different rhythmically:

Upper part dissonant portamento; middle part consonant portamento

Upper part ornamentation; middle part consonant

P. Ex. 27. 11

P. Ex. 66. 8

P. Ex. 211. 11-12

An interesting example of double Cambiatas in different rhythm against a portamento.

EIGHTH NOTES

Review Chapters 21 and 23.

With few exceptions, eighth note pairs occur on the second half of the beat (as passing tones or auxiliary notes). Their agreement with moving parts depends on their own way of moving.

Scalewise up or down either of the two notes may be consonant or dissonant with the prevailing harmony; but the first eighth note is usually consonant with a moving quarter note in another part (see Ex. 23, 21 and 25; 71, 35).

There are some exceptions (as in the three following examples against unaccented passing tones):

Simultaneous pairs of eighth notes usually move in thirds:

Both pairs in a scale line   Both with change of direction

One pair in scale line, the other changing direction

Musica ficta occasionally causes augmented and diminished intervals to occur between eighth notes and other parts.

See further, Ex. 31, 74; 33, 102; 71, 13 (the last in quarter notes).

Either of the eighth notes as an upper auxiliary is of extremely rare occurrence (see Ex. 175, 42).

The validity of the rule of agreement between the lowest part and each of the upper parts is beyond question. General practice confirms this opinion. Dissonant clashes between the upper parts and between the upper parts and the lowest part occur in the manner shown in this chapter; an indiscriminate use of dissonance, even if in agreement with the lowest part, cannot be tolerated.

Assignment: The student should familiarize himself with the material in each section in turn. A theme of his own invention, or one chosen from *Examples*, should be used alternately in either of three parts, adding the two other parts in free counterpoint. Apply the devices contained in this chapter in the order presented.

Chapter 37.

The Consonant Fourth

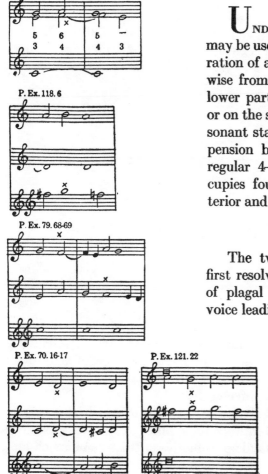

P. Ex. 118. 6

P. Ex. 79. 68-69

P. Ex. 70. 16-17   P. Ex. 121. 22

Under certain conditions the perfect fourth may be used as a consonance in the chord of preparation of a suspension. It is then approached stepwise from above or from below over a sustained lower part. The fourth, occurring on the fourth or on the second beat as a consonance, is given dissonant status by the adding of a fifth on the suspension beat; the fourth is then resolved as a regular 4–3 suspension. The device always occupies four half note beats, and is used in interior and deceptive as well as final cadences.

The two consecutive consonant fourths (the first resolved irregularly) give the texture a kind of plagal cadence effect. Notice the interesting voice leading.

Occasionally the fourth is doubled: Both fourths are approached by step, the doubled fourth here being a half note lower auxiliary (in no other case allowed, except in fast triple time).

P. Ex. 84. 179

The doubled fourth is a regular half note passing tone.

P. Ex. 117. 15

This example shows the consonant fourth in reverse; the fourth occurs between the sustained top voice and another upper voice as well as the lower part, the doubled fourth, G, moving as a half note passing tone to the dissonant note A.

Study the following examples: Ex. 23, 28; 63, 64; 48, 28; 114, 51; 117, 20.

Assignment: Using an approach of at least a measure, write consonant fourths on all white notes of the keyboard and B flat; on F, substitute B flat for B; on B flat, E flat substitutes for E. End with regular cadences and endeavor to make the voice leading as interesting as possible. When using a deceptive cadence continue the texture for another measure.

Chapter 38.

The Regular Form of the $\frac{6}{5}$ Chord

THE sixth added to the fifth or the fifth added to the sixth creates the dissonance of a second or a seventh. This dissonance was generally treated as a suspension. On the other hand, freedom of movement, because of the consonant character with the bass, is encountered quite frequently.

The simultaneous occurrence of the sixth and the fifth over a bass note may be observed as early as the thirteenth century in organum. The conscious recognition of the harmonic as well as the melodic possibilities of the $\frac{6}{5}$ came much later and attained more variety in the sixteenth century.

The common, or what may be called the regular, form of the $^6_5$ (in later styles the cadence formula II $^6_5$ v I) was treated as a suspension.   A number of variations may be observed:

a) Regular:

> The fifth (perfect) prepared on beats two or four.
> The sixth (major or minor) enters freely and remains stationary.
> The fifth resolves down by step on beats two or four.
> The bass rises by step simultaneously with the downward step of the resolution, forming a major or a minor triad.

This form of the $^6_5$ chord shared the location on beats one and three with the common suspension dissonance, and had the same preparation and resolution beats, i.e., two or four.

The resolution of the $^6_5$ may be simple or ornamented.

The last ornamented resolution is sometimes found in augmentation; here the note of resolution may be analyzed as an accented passing tone:

The regular $^6_5$ is used in interior cadences as well as in texture without cadential significance. (The final cadence of a composition prefers the regular 4–3 or 9–8 suspensions.)   The $^6_5$ often leads into a deceptive cadence.

Study the following examples:

> P. Ex. 23, 19–20   Cadential
> P. Ex. 47, 9   Noncadential
> P. Ex. 45, 26–27   Deceptive
> P. Ex. 99, 79   Deceptive
> P. Ex. 31, 74–75   Embellished
> P. Ex. 69, 29   In augmentation (in final cadences)
> P. Ex. 74, 15   In augmentation

b) Regular except for the sixth moving up stepwise parallel with the bass, the chord of resolution forming the first inversion of a triad:

See P. Ex. 97, 12.

c) Regular except for the bass skipping down a third under the resolution:

See P. Ex. 97, 11.

d) Regular except for the bass skipping down a fifth under the resolution:

e) Regular; the lowest note on the first beat is A in the first tenor; it becomes F under the resolution, thus actually producing the effect of a skip of a sixth upwards:

f) Regular; the resolution triad is diminished. B in the lower part is a half note passing tone against F.

g) The fifth is diminished. Otherwise the device is regular.

De Monte, *Liber Quartus Motettorum,* Motet I, p. 3, m. 24.

This form of $\frac{6}{5}$ is of comparatively rare occurrence.

Chapter 39.

The $\frac{6}{5}$ Chord Combined with the Consonant Fourth

THE $\frac{6}{5}$ is prepared as usual, but the bass remains stationary which causes a consonant fourth to be formed on the resolution beat. The consonant fourth then is treated in the usual manner (see Chapter 37).

The $\frac{6}{5}$ combined with the consonant fourth is a standard cadence formula in the style.

The foregoing examples all had the fifth prepared and the sixth added; the reverse will be illustrated in the following chapter.

Chapter 40.

The $\frac{6}{5}$ Chord with the Sixth Prepared and the Fifth Added

THE sixth progresses into the fifth. The weakness of this device is evident. It was offset, in most cases, by a stronger suspension dissonance on the next strong beat, or by adding a prepared suspension dissonance (the fourth) to the $\frac{6}{5}$.

P. Ex. 140 16-17

A $\frac{6}{5}$ followed by a regular 4–3 suspension on the next strong beat.
See also P. Ex. 55, m. 33.

P. Vol. XXIII. 89. 2. 2

A similar example; notice the use of the Nota Cambiata. (In both examples the sixth goes into the fifth on the second half of the suspension beat.)

De Monte; Requiem p. 11. m. 13

A 9–8 suspension follows the $\frac{6}{5}$: the fifth prepares the 9–8 suspension.

P. Ex. 101. 115-16

P. A. M. Jahrgang 9· Willaert
6. Domine Jesu Christe. p. 9. m. 59

P. Ex. 200. 6-7

P. Ex. 209. 42-3

A 7–6 suspension follows the $\frac{6}{5}$: the fifth prepares the 7–6 suspension. A frequent device.

See also P. Ex. 62, m. 25–26
107, 18
136, 16
185, 8
200, 48.

The first $\frac{6}{5}$ resolves to a first inversion followed by a regular $\frac{6}{5}$. Notice the movement of the bass.

The $\frac{6}{5}$ is followed by a triad on the next odd beat instead of a suspension. This procedure is comparatively infrequent. See also P. Ex. p. 204, m. 93; the $\frac{6}{5}$ is here followed by a first inversion of a triad.

So far all $\frac{6}{5}$ chords were placed on odd, i.e., strong, beats.

Occasionally a $\frac{6}{5}$ with the sixth prepared and the fifth added is found on even, i.e., weak, beats, serving as a preparation for a regular suspension dissonance; the fifth then prepares the dissonance, and the sixth remains.

See also P. Ex. 210, 51; 209, 29.

Chapter 41.

Free Treatment of the $\frac{6}{5}$ Chord

THE examples quoted are extremely rare. The basic theory of composition in the sixteenth century, i.e., consonant agreement with the bass, is evident always; dissonance between the upper parts is treated with extreme caution. Most of these examples may be considered as experimental.

Pierre Certon: Mass "Regnum Mundi"
(From Renaissance to Baroque
Benedictus p. 79. m. 1-4)

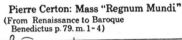

Both the fifth and the sixth enter stepwise; the fifth remains as preparation for another $\frac{6}{5}$, the fifth of which skips to third instead of resolving in the usual manner. In the third appearance of the $\frac{6}{5}$ the fifth and the sixth are approached and left by step.

Willaert: Motet "Domine Jesu Christe
(P.A.M. Jahrgang 9. p. 12. m. 201-2)

The sixth is approached by step, the fifth enters after a rest. Both are left by step.

Samin: Mass Sancte Spiritus: Sanctus   Le Heurter: Mass Osculetor Me; Gloria
(Stein's Thesis Vol. I. p. 117. m. 14)   (Stein's Thesis Vol. I. p. 165. m. 8)

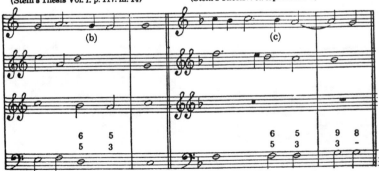

P. De Monte. Liber Quartus Motettorum
No. 6. p. 27 m. 5.

The fifth is prepared and resolved as a half note passing tone at *a*), as a quarter note passing tone at *b*) and *c*).

P. Ex. 139. 70-2

P. Ex. 191. 70-1

P. Ex. 138. 51-3

The fifth and the sixth enter and leave by skip or step. Extremely rare.

Chapter 42.

The $\frac{6}{5}$ Chord Occurring on Half Beats · Sequential Treatment

THE unprepared $\frac{6}{5}$ occurring briefly on the first or the second half of the beat deserves mention, if for no other reason than to remove doubt from the mind of the student.

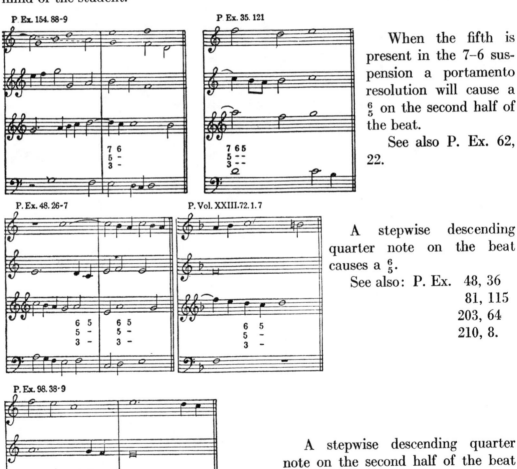

When the fifth is present in the 7–6 suspension a portamento resolution will cause a $\frac{6}{5}$ on the second half of the beat.

See also P. Ex. 62, 22.

A stepwise descending quarter note on the beat causes a $\frac{6}{5}$.

See also: P. Ex. 48, 36
                  81, 115
                203, 64
                210, 8.

A stepwise descending quarter note on the second half of the beat causes a $\frac{6}{5}$.

P. De Monte. Liber Quartus Motettorum
No. 9. p. 43. m. 14-15

A stepwise ascending quarter note causes a $^6_5$.

P. De Monte.
(Oberg's Thesis: Part I, p. 142)

The skip from G to E in the alto causes a $^6_5$ on the second half of the beat.

Nearly all of these examples have the dissonance between the fifth and the sixth approached stepwise in a descending line, especially when the clash occurs on the beat. In the latter case it seems to follow the law of the accented quarter note passing tone. The author has not found any example in an ascending line.

SEQUENTIAL TREATMENT OF THE $^6_5$

P. Vol. XV. 13. 4. 3

The example quoted is rare.

Chapter 43.

The $\frac{6}{5}$ Chord in Triple Time

THE $\frac{6}{5}$ occurs infrequently in triple time. The $\frac{3}{2}$ and $\frac{3}{1}$ which indicate fast triple time change occurring in certain portions of the Gloria, the Credo, the Sanctus, and in some other compositions, generally employ the larger note values, and are often homophonic in character. The suspension dissonances are found more frequently on beats two and three than on one. The evidence regarding the use of the $\frac{6}{5}$ in triple time is not too conclusive from the examples quoted, but they may serve as a guide in general. The author has found none on the second beat; the ones quoted are on the first and on the third beats.

P. Vol. X. 50. 3. 7-8

Time signature $\frac{3}{2}$.

The preparation and the resolution are regular; the $\frac{6}{5}$ occurs on the third beat and the resolution on the first.

P. Ex. 115. 90-1

Time signature $\frac{3}{1}$.

The sixth is prepared on the third beat. The portamento resolution into the fifth prepares the 7–6 suspension following (compare P. 101, 115–16, Chapter 40).

P Vol V 87.2 4-5

P. Ex. 110. 28-9.

This example is taken from the motet *Tollite jugum meum* which is in $\frac{3}{1}$ time in its entirety. All note values are used, which indicates a moderate tempo. The $\frac{6}{5}$ occurs on the first beat, the fifth is prepared and resolved in the regular manner, but the bass skips an octave, crossing the tenor part under the resolution, producing the effect of ascending skip of a sixth (compare Section *e* of the $\frac{6}{5}$, Chapter 38).

Time signature $\frac{3}{1}$.

The fifth is prepared (by a portamento-like consonance), the sixth enters by step and continues down into the fifth which prepares a 7-6 suspension. In Jeppesen's *The Style of Palestrina and the Dissonance*, pages 101–2, there is a reference to this example. The $\frac{6}{5}$ dissonance on the first beat is termed a breach of style; by rebarring the measure and halving the note values he arrives at a plausible style analysis. A different analysis is suggested: All parts agree consonantly with the bass which is, after all, the basis of the style; this fact alone would seem sufficient to justify this dissonance as it stands, even if the previous review of the $\frac{6}{5}$, would not show its further justification. (Compare the preceding example.)

Chapter 44.

Three-Part Exercises with Canonic Imitation in Two of the Parts • Augmentation and Mirroring • Imitation in Three Parts

As a gradual introduction to imitation in three parts, the following examples should be analyzed and similar exercises should be written.

1. The two upper parts in canonic imitation, the lower part in free counterpoint. Cadence on the final. Write in the free part simultaneously with the two other parts. Customary dissonances may occur between the two upper parts, but each upper part must agree with the lowest part. Interrupt the canon before the cadence in all these exercises:

Dorian

2. The lower and the middle parts in canonic imitation, the top part free. The upper two parts must agree, as usual, with the lowest part. Cadence on the final.

Mixolydian

3. The two extreme parts in canonic imitation, the middle part free. Cadence on the final:

Phrygian

4. Like 1, 2, or 3. In two sections, the first ending in a hocket cadence proper to the mode (not the final), and the second section ending on the final. Use augmentation in the first section and mirroring in the second section:

Dorian

Since augmentation doubles the length of the theme it cannot be augmented for its whole length in this case, but must be interrupted at a convenient point (*a*).

The mirroring is interrupted at *b* because of the cadence.

Neither augmentation nor mirroring needs to be conducted for any definite length. A few measures usually will be sufficient.

5. Imitation in three parts. Cadence on the final. The imitation may be interrupted at a convenient point (after about two measures, or more). The melodic line is then conducted in free counterpoint until a suitable cadence is reached:

Dorian

Chapter 45.

Triple Counterpoint

IN TRIPLE counterpoint each part is invertible. It follows that six ways are possible; the following numbers, read perpendicularly, represent the voice parts:

$$1\ 1\ 2\ 2\ 3\ 3$$
$$2\ 3\ 1\ 3\ 1\ 2$$
$$3\ 2\ 3\ 1\ 2\ 1$$

The only practical inversion interval is that of the octave. The fifth and the fourth may be used as passing tones only. Consequently, first inversions are available with a doubled bass or a doubled sixth. The suspensions 7–6, 2–3, and 4–3 are possible only if the bass note is doubled.

The remaining consonances are unisons, thirds, sixths, and octaves. All three parts must be in consonant agreement with each other. Use contrary and oblique motion in order to avoid hidden octaves.

The following examples are written in triple counterpoint at the octave. The invertible counterpoint is interrupted at *a* and in the inverted example at *b* because of the cadence:

Examples of triple counterpoint are fairly uncommon in the style. When they occur they are mostly of brief duration or quite free.

Chapter 46.

Thematic and Harmonic Analysis of Three-Part Compositions

THE sixteenth-century vocal compositions were usually in sectional form, and in fugal or canonic or sometimes homophonic style.

The composition chosen for analysis is part of the hymn *In Dominicis Quadragesima*, Ex. p. 155.

The sectioning is done by numbers according to the division of the text. Each section is, so to say, the first exposition of a fugue, which is succeeded, in turn, by another exposition, and so on. When the thematic material is not imitated, it should be labeled as free counterpoint. The text of a section is sometimes repeated; in such a case it receives the same number with an added letter.

The composition below is in sectional fugal style (see Chapter 31).

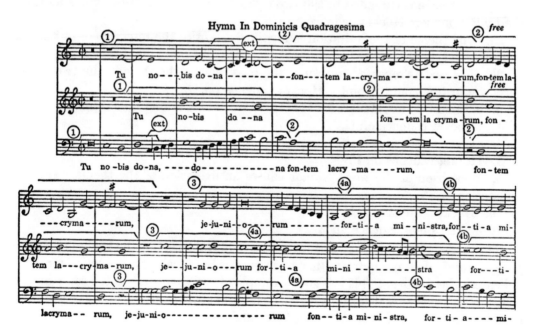

Hymn In Dominicis Quadragesima

THEMATIC ANALYSIS

1. The theme is extended in the two extreme parts. The initial notes indicate the Lydian mode. Hocket cadence on C.

2*a*. The theme of the imitation is modified. Notice the intervals of imitation. Hocket cadence on D.

2*b*. The text is repeated, but only the bass repeats the theme; the two upper parts are in free counterpoint. Hocket cadence on G.

3. This section dovetails with section 4*a* without a strong intervening cadence.

4*a*. Hocket cadence on C.

4*b*. Hocket cadence on C.

5. Hocket cadence on F.

6. Repetition of the word *retunde* causes an extension of the theme. Hocket cadence on C.

7*a*. Hocket cadence on C.

7*b* and *c*. Final cadence on A.

The mode is the Aeolian according to the final cadence, but the beginning of the piece certainly does not indicate this mode, just as practically every section strongly indicates other modes. This is a good example of the vagueness in the sense of key which often makes a definite key analysis difficult. Notice the variety of the initial notes of the themes: A, C, D, E, F, and G.

HARMONIC ANALYSIS

Chords are indicated by letters: major by capital letters; minor by small letters; diminished by small letters and a zero; augmented by capital letters and a plus.

Suspension dissonances are analyzed as separate chords only if there is a chord change at the resolution; otherwise they are analyzed by their resolution; $^6_5$ chords are analyzed as first inversions of seventh chords; chords with doubled bass notes and the sixth present are analyzed as first inversions, as are those with the sixth doubled; the consonant fourth is analyzed as the second inversion of a triad.

This procedure has been adopted for practical reasons only. In general, the lowest note will indicate the letter in cases of ambiguity.

The following is a harmonic analysis of the hymn. Analysis by duration and progression is followed by a summary of root movement. In general, such an index tends to show the most prevalent chords in any given mode; practically every composition contained in *Examples* shows a prevalence of the important chords in each mode, i.e., the dominant, subdominant, and the chord on the final.

The numbers indicate measures; the dots, half note time units:

```
1              2           3           4           5           6           7           8
· · · · · · · | · · · · | · · · · | · · · · | · · · · | · · · · | · · · · | · · · · |
           d     F  C     G  dF    aC G    Ca  e   G  f♯°   G  d a
   9        10      11       12      13      14      15      16     17
· · · · | · · · · | · · · · | · · · · | · · · · | · · · · | · · · · | · · · · |
F⁷ d A     d      a   F b° e   D  G    G   a    aC G    a   F   Ce C F  d CF⁷G
   18       19      20       21      22      23      24      25      26
· · · · | · · · · | · · · · | · · · · | · · · · | · · · · | · · · · | · · · · |
C   G     C  G     C  F G   F dC    GaG    Ca  e   dFG    F    C  d  C
   27       28      29       30      31      32      33      34      35
· · · · | · · · · | · · · · | · · · · | · · · · | · · · · | · · · · | · · · · |
F         CF b°C   d F      a F G    C   G    CF   C   F   d a   d    a   GCd⁷G
   36       37      38       39      40      41
· · · · | · · · · | · · · · | · · · · | · · · · | · · · · ‖
C   aG   a     d   G⁷a d    dad      d  E    A
```

This gives the following duration frequency:

G 31, C 29, d 26, F26, a23, A6, e5, b° 2, D 2, E 2, f♯° 2, F⁷ 2 G⁷ I, d⁷ I, a total of 158 beats.

Chord Movements	Root Movements	
C to F G a d e d⁷	5th up	22
21 6 7 3 2 1 1		
G to C a d F f♯°	4th up	28
18 9 4 2 2 1		
d to a F C A G⁷ E	3rd up	10
15 5 4 3 1 1 1		
a to d e F G C F⁷	3rd down	12
15 4 2 3 3 2 1		
F to C d G a b°	2nd up	15
15 5 3 3 2 2		
e to G D C d	2nd down	11
4 1 1 1 1		
F⁷ to d G		98

2   1 1
d ^{7} to G
1   1
f#° to G
1   1
A to d
1   1
b ° to e C
2   1 1
D to G
1   1
E to a
1   1
G^7 to a
1   1
—
98

It is interesting to note that the triad on the dominant E occurs only five times while the subdominant triad occurs seventeen times, thus confirming the tendency of favoring the latter in the Aeolian mode.

Strict canonic style is exemplified in the "Benedictus" from the Mass *Ad Fugam*, Ex. p. 90. This is a canon "three in one," i.e., strict imitation in three parts. There are three expositions, each with a different subject. Uninterrupted continuity, with not a single strong cadential punctuation, characterizes this composition.

FUGUE

Compositions with repeated words sometimes show a more extended use of the fugal idea in that a counter-exposition may occur in stretto. In the Benedictus (Ex. p. 70) the first exposition is followed by a counter-exposition in stretto, and the second section (in nomine Domini) shows several stretti. This is about as far as the vocal composers went in fugue composition.

Chapter 47

Three-Part Counterpoint with Text

Some of the shorter texts of the Mass (see Chapter 52) should be chosen for setting, such as the Benedictus or the Agnus Dei. They are generally set in duple $\frac{4}{2}$ time.

SUGGESTIONS FOR ASSIGNMENTS

1. Three-part imitation without textual repetition, like the following example:

The division of the text in this example is in three sections:

   a) Benedictus. A hocket cadence on A ends the section.

   b) qui venit.

   c) in nomine Domini. The second and the third sections dovetail, with a light cadence on C in measure 8. Final cadence on D.

2. Canonic imitation in two of the parts, free imitation in the third part. The Benedictus, Ex. p. 166, has been chosen as a pattern.

THEMATIC ANALYSIS

First section:

   Canon at the unison between the two altos: the word *Benedictus* (1*a*) and subsequent repetitions are set to different themes (1*b*) (1*c*).

   The soprano: the word *Benedictus* (1*a*) and subsequent repetitions (1*b*) (1*c*) in free imitation. The section ends with a hocket cadence on G in measure 14.

Second section:

   The canon: the first *qui venit* (2*a*, measure 12–13) dovetails with the first section, taking part in the cadence on G. Subsequent repetitions (2*b*) (2*c*) follow. The soprano: qui venit occurs three times using variations of 2*a*.

Third section:

   The canon: the words *in nomine Domini* (3*a*, measure 23) dovetail with the second section without strong cadential punctuation. Light, passing cadences may be observed in measures 23 and 26. Subsequent repetitions (3*a*, measure

25) (3b, from measure 31 onward) follow in varied forms until the end. The soprano: the first *in nomine Domini* (3b, measure 28) is followed by repetitions in free and, in places, fragmentary imitation.

The sign ⅍ (measures 4 and 43) indicates the entrance of the follower. The sign ⌒ (measure 43) indicates the end of the leader. The subsequent first alto entrance (measure 44) serves to take part in the coda and as a filling-in part.

3. Fugal exposition with counter-expositions similar to the Benedictus on page 70 of *Examples*.

ANALYSIS

First section: exposition (measures 1–12).

    Counter-exposition in stretto (measures 10–17) ending on a clausula vera cadence on D (between the cantus and the alto).

    Episodical treatment begins in the tenor (measure 16) with free counterpoint in the cantus and a fragment of the theme of the first section, with extension, in the alto. The section ends in measure 22.

Second section:

    The exposition (new theme) begins in measure 21.

    A series of counter-expositions in stretto begins in measure 28, ending with a short coda (measures 43–44).

This piece is characterized by constant dovetailing of themes without strong cadential punctuation.

4. Canon three in one.

        First section: (1a) Benedictus.
                    (1b) qui venit.
        Second section: (2a) in nomine Domini, (measure 8).
                    (2b) in nomine Domini, (measure 14).

The 2b theme is designed with the object of making possible a final cadence (see the cantus, measure 16, and the imitation in the tenor, measure 20).

The cantus fills in with free counterpoint (measures 19–21). The imitation intervals (the fifth below, in its turn followed by another fifth) greatly facilitate the strict imitation. For customary divisions of the Agnus Dei, see *Examples*.

PART FOUR

Counterpoint in Four and More Parts

Chapter 48.

Four-Part Homophonic Writing · Declamatory Style

I<small>N THE</small> sixteenth century a movement to reform certain practices in both the performance and the style of church music was initiated in ecclesiastical circles.* Among other things, severe criticism had been directed for some time towards the overly florid style of composition which prevented the understanding of the text. The result of the reform was a gradual union of contrapuntal and homophonic styles in ecclesiastical music.

FOUR-PART HOMOPHONIC WRITING

The free prose meter was preserved in the musical settings. The text was literally *declaimed*; while in polyphony each part had its own secondary rhythm, homophonic style had one *collective* rhythm, as it were, all voices generally changing syllable simultaneously.

This declamatory style, alternating with contrapuntal style, is found in the longer movements of the Mass, i.e., in the Gloria and the Credo, and in motets and other types of church music such as the Lamentations by Palestrina and the Responses by Ingegneri, (Ex. 214–225).

HARMONY

The purely harmonic aspect of compositions in homophonic as well as contrapuntal style should be explored because of its dissimilarity with the later development of harmony. The modes were not used in their *pure* form, because chromaticism (musica ficta) had invaded the field. The consequence was not that of modulation in the modern sense, but rather that of harmonic color without a definite feeling of key.

The following composition by Lassus (from the Penitential Psalms, Vol. IV, 85, 2, 1) is a good illustration:

---

* See Lang's *Music in Western Civilization*, p. 229.

The final cadence indicates the Phrygian mode. The beginning points to the Mixolydian mode, the cadence on G being in common to the two modes. Later a Phrygian cadence is followed by one on D and another on G (plagal). The B flat major chord adds another touch of color.

Other compositions recommended for study: Palestrina: *Veni Sancte Spiritu* (Ex. 36); Ingegneri: Responses (Ex. 214–225).

CADENCES

Chapter 32 and further study of the examples indicated below will be sufficient to illustrate the use of cadences:

Authentic: with the octave in the upper part: Ex. 36, 7–8; 47, 18–19;
with the third in the upper part: Ex. 36, 12–13; 78, 64–65;
with the fifth in the upper part: Ex. 38, 63–64; 217, 27–28.

Plagal: with the octave in the upper voice: Ex. 24, 60–61; 50, 76–77;.
with the third in the upper voice: Ex. 39, 92–93; 52, 33–34;
with the fifth in the upper voice: Ex. 43, 131–132; 83, 169–170.

Phrygian: Ex. 46, 43–44.

Deceptive: see Chapter 32.

The raised note (the modern leading tone) in the initial cadence chord may be approached:

a) stepwise from above (frequent because of the conventional suspension to the raised note). Ex. 20, 6.

b) stepwise from below (less frequent). Ex. 33, 91.

c) by a descending skip of a third. Ex. 24, 52; 77, 26.

d) by an ascending skip of a third. P. Vol. IV, 47, 1–2.

The raised note in the initial cadence chord usually proceeds stepwise upwards to the final. Rare instances of skips may be found: a third down, Ex. 74, 22, a fourth up, Ex. 96, 73.

In changes of position of the same chord in which the raised note is present, it may be approached and left by an ascending or a descending skip of a third. Such changes of position are infrequent, however; when they occur, the change is to the adjacent position of the chord, either upwards or downwards (Ex. 23, 27–28, 40, 106).

Examples of the approach to the raised third of the final cadence chord:

In the authentic cadence:

Skip from the octave to the raised third: Ex. 23, 29; 38, 67–68.

The same skip abridged by a passing seventh: Ex. 36, 12–13.

The fifth to the raised third by an upward step: Ex. 36, 7–8.

The clausula vera type of cadence deprives the authentic cadence of its third in the final chord (Ex. 39, 83–84).

In the plagal cadence:

The octave by step downwards to the raised third: Ex. 24, 61; 43, 131–132.

The sixth by step upwards to the raised third: Ex. 43, 131–132 (Chorus II).

In the Phrygian cadence:

The third by step downwards to the raised third: Ex. 46, 43–44.

OTHER OBSERVATIONS

1. Parallel octaves and fifths are forbidden.

2. Exposed or hidden octaves occur most frequently at cadences, when the upper note of the octave is approached by step and the lower note by skip in the same direction (see Ex. 38, 51–52; 38, 67–68). They are always good wherever they occur. Octaves approached by skip in the same direction in both parts should be avoided in four parts; they are more likely to be found in six or seven parts, and in double or triple chorus compositions (Ex. 126, 40).

3. Exposed fifths are more frequent. They may occur between any of the parts:

   a) the upper part an ascending step, the lower part an ascending skip (Ex. 36, 3–4).

   b) the upper part a descending skip, the lower part a descending step (Ex. 34, 106).

   c) the upper part a descending step, the lower part a descending skip (Ex. 39, 79).

   d) the upper part an ascending skip, the lower part an ascending step (Ex. 169, 22). To be used only in texture of more than four parts.

Skips in the same direction in both parts should be avoided (see Ex. 74, 21–22; 86, 199, *dead interval;* 119, 24).

4. For the best sonority close spacing is recommended. Do not exceed the distance of an octave between the parts except between the bass and the next upper part in homophonic style.

5. The text is usually divided according to the punctuation. Textual repetition is sometimes a matter of choice, or emphasis, or musical necessity.
Cadences should be used according to the importance of the punctuation.

6. Musical accents (agogic) should coincide with the metrical accents of the text as far as possible.

7. Use the Latin texts, or their English translations found in the back of *Examples*.

8. Always write each voice on a separate staff.

Assignment:

Write a Response in four parts. It may be done for either women's or men's voices, or for mixed chorus.

For a pattern the Response (Ex. pp. 224–225) No. 32 by Ingegneri has been chosen. It is in the transposed Phrygian mode on B. While most of these Responses are in an abbreviated three-part form, No. 32 is in a complete three-part form: the first part ending with "ejus," is followed by the second part (the Verse) in three voices, after which there is a return to "Et erit in pace memoria ejus," followed by a complete repetition of the first part, ending on "ejus."

The cadence at the end of the first part must be on the final of the mode. The cadence at the end of the "Verse" must be chosen so as to fit the return to "Et erit," etc.; likewise the beginning of the first part should be a logical continuation from the final cadence of the piece.

Responses No. 21 and No. 23 are in the Lydian mode with the final cadence on F. This is unusual; the conventional Lydian generally had B flat in the key signature, if the final was on F.

Chapter 49.

Florid Style · Four-Part Counterpoint Containing a Two-Part Canon

THE first part of this chapter deals with counterpoint in free florid style without imitation. Sufficient guidance in regard to cadences is found in the previous chapter.

In addition to the rules for the use of suspensions contained in Chapter 35 the following observations are pertinent:

1. The 7–6 suspension: besides the dissonance the third and the fifth may be present (a complete seventh chord). Observe the general rule regarding the treatment of the fifth (Ex. 35, 121; 29, 29).

The following doublings may occur: the third (Ex. 34, 118); the bass note doubled in an upper voice (Ex. 147, 9; 149, 35). The fifth is the least likely interval to be doubled in four parts.

Additional examples:

> Ex. 33, 96: Change of bass.
> Ex. 46, 43: Parallel fourths.
> Ex. 47, 16: The fifth ascending to the sixth.
> Ex. 51, 6: Change of bass, interesting voice leading.
> Ex. 74, 31: Ornamented resolution and simultaneous movement of the fifth.
> Ex. 208, 9; 210, 8: The fifth remains stationary.

The dissonant seventh may be placed in any of the upper parts.

2. The 2–3 suspension:

In four parts the variations of treatment are not so frequent as those in three parts.

> Resolution to a first inversion: Ex. 22, 11; 66, 22.
> Resolution to a triad (notice the change of bass through the addition of a lower part): Ex. 117, 28.

3. The 4–3 suspension:

Besides the fourth the following intervals occur: the octave and the fifth, or the octave and the sixth.

See the following examples:

Ex. 24, 58: The fourth is augmented, the bass moves down a third.

Ex. 29, 35: Notice the passing seventh causing parallel fourths with the resolution.

Ex. 50, 74: Interesting voice leading.

The dissonant fourth may be placed in any of the upper parts.

4. The 9–8 suspension:

Besides the dissonance the fifth and the third are present: see Ex. 25, 68 and 46, 38 (change of bass through the entrance of another part). In general, the chord of resolution should be a complete triad with the fundamental doubled. The dissonant ninth may be placed in any of the upper parts.

Assignment:

Write a short, rhythmically interesting melody ending in a cadence point. Add three parts in free contrapuntal style. The following examples illustrate the alternate use of the same theme in two voices.

FOUR-PART COUNTERPOINT CONTAINING A TWO-PART CANON

The canon may be placed in any two parts. The last measure of the leader is usually designed so as to permit a cadence at the end of the follower. The two added parts are in free contrapuntal style. A short coda follows, ending with a cadence.

The following example illustrates the use of a canon at the fifth above, between the tenor and the alto:

The same canon inverted at the octave (not, however, in double counterpoint) between the soprano and the alto:

Assignment:

Write exercises similar to the above examples. For further practice, place the canon in different voices.

Chapter 50.

Four-Part Imitation Without Text . Quadruple Counterpoint

THE initial sections of four-part polyphonic compositions will be used as models for preliminary exercises in four-part imitation. The types enumerated below have been chosen with this object in view.

The theme should be interesting rhythmically as well as melodically; it should have identity of its own, as it were. Adjacent imitations usually enter at the distance of a fourth or a fifth, but other intervals may be used, among which the unison is frequent. The initial notes usually represent the final and the dominant, thus expressing the mode, but occasionally other initials may be found.

There is, naturally, a great deal of choice as regards the temporal distance between the imitations. Close imitation (stretto) was a general characteristic of the style.

Analysis of the first sections of the following compositions will show different types of imitation:

1. Ex. 140: Canonic imitation in stretto in two parts, followed by an exact restatement in the remaining two parts. The counterpoint uses thematic material and free treatment (in the Netherland tradition).

2. Ex. 44: Two parts in canonic imitation. The entrance of the fourth part is delayed.

3. Ex. 46: Imitations enter at regular intervals of measures.

4. Ex. 51: Imitation in mirroring.

5. Ex. 76: A duet in mirroring followed by a restatement in the other parts.

6. Ex. 52: The four initial entrances in extremely close stretto.

7. Ex. 164: Two different themes are used in the first section. The second part begins in measure 28.

8. Ex. 87–92: From the Mass *Ad Fugam*. Canonic imitation throughout.

Assignment:

1. Short exercises in four-part imitation ending in a cadence proper to the mode similar to the example below. The imitations need to be exact only up to the entrance of the next voice:

The last entrance, in this case the bass, is sometimes shortened for cadential reasons.

2. Exercises in two sections, the first section ending with a cadence. The new theme of the second section dovetails with the end of the first section, generally taking part in the cadence and continuing beyond. Any of the sections previously enumerated may serve as models.

QUADRUPLE COUNTERPOINT.

Review Chapters 28 and 45.

No additional rules are necessary. The only practical inversion is that of the octave. Twenty-four inversions are possible.

Suggestions for assignments:

1. Texture in four parts without imitation.

2. Imitation reverting to free treatment after the last entrance (but still in quadruple counterpoint).

3. Two different themes, in imitation, for example:

  S. 1
  A. 2
  T. 1
  B. 2

or other combinations.

4. Canon four in one (see examples):

Canon four in one in quadruple counterpoint:

The same canon in inversion:

Chapter 51.

The Writing of a Complete Motet with Text

THE motet and the Mass may be considered to be the most important polyphonic vocal compositions of religious character in the sixteenth century.

The early motet was a sacred polyphonic composition which originated about the beginning of the thirteenth century. It underwent many changes up to its final period (about 1750). Its greatest development was reached in the sixteenth century.

Excerpts from the Vulgate (the translation to Latin of the Bible) and religious poems were used as textual material. The musical form was sectional; each division of the text was set to different thematic material of imitative or homophonic character, the latter serving as transitions between the former. The procedure is similar to what we now call *through composed* style as far as the continued change of new thematic material is concerned; it was prevalent in all vocal compositions of the period, ecclesiastical as well as secular.

There are some rare exceptions, among which is Palestrina's motet *Alleluia Tulerunt* (Ex. 147) in which the Alleluia theme is interpolated between sections of different thematic material, resulting in the following scheme: A B A C A D A E A (akin to an extended rondo form).

The following motets are recommended as models for writing:

1. Dies Sanctificatus (Ex. 140).
   The textual division is as follows:
   a) Dies sanctificatus illuxit nobis (measures 1–18)
   b) Venite gentes et adorate Dominum (measures 18–36)
   c) Quia hodie descendit lux magna in terris (measures 37–52)
   d) Haec dies quam fecit Dominus (measures 52–67)
   e) Exultemus et laetemur in ea. (measures 68–89).

Section 1.

The theme is divided in two parts: (a) Measures 1–4, soprano, and (b), measures 4–10. The imitation is canonic; the subsequent restatement in the two lower parts is exact except for a slight change at the cadence. The thematic material of the counterpoint is partly free and partly drawn from the principal themes. The initial notes of the theme and its imitation serve as the bass for the cadence D to A (measures 8–9).

Section 2.

This section is divided in two parts: (a), measures 18–37 on the words *Venite gentes*, and (b), measures 27–36 on the words *et adorate Dominum.*

a) The theme enters in the bass. Note the simultaneous rhythmic imitation in the soprano and in the tenor. The alto and the tenor imitate at the unison, the latter in stretto, followed by the soprano at the octave. The section ends with another entrance by the bass; in both bass themes the first note is in augmentation.

b) The thematic material is derived from that of *a* and is at first introduced as counterpoint (during *a*) in the alto (measure 24). It is the augmentation of the latter part of *a*. In subsequent entrances there is a great deal of freedom, especially in the treatment of the first skip and that of the rhythm.

Section 3.

After a brief homophonic section (notice the stepwise harmonic progressions) on Quia hodie, the new theme enters on the word *descendit*. Here is an example of graphic illustration occasionally used in Gregorian chant as well as in polyphonic vocal compositions. Only the descending skip of the fifth is imitated, after which all voices continue in free counterpoint.

Section 4.

The theme is based on the Gregorian Gradual "Haec dies" (*Liber Usualis*, page 688):

A duet (canonic) between the alto (measure 52) and the soprano is followed by a duet between the tenor and the bass in partial augmentation. Fragments of the principal theme and free counterpoint are used as counter-themes. The soprano repeats the theme (measure 61) closing the section.

Section 5.

The section changes to triple time. Such changes of meter occur with relative frequency in certain movements of the Mass and in other compositions. The following explanation of the *proportional system* (the proportional time value of notes under different time signatures) is here meant to be applied to a few cases only. Since we deal with music already transcribed, the question of the relative tempo of the music in which different time signatures are involved is the only issue of importance for our purpose.

There was a tendency towards simplification of the proportional system in the sixteenth century; the most generally used signature for duple time became ¢ (alla breve) in which the unit of time, tactus (measure), was represented by the brevis. Each tactus had two whole note beats:*

$$ ¢ \quad \underset{\text{depressio}}{\downarrow} \quad \underset{\text{elevatio}}{\uparrow} $$

The change to triple meter was expressed by certain arithmetic ratios (only $\frac{3}{1}$ and $\frac{3}{2}$ will be considered here).

The $\frac{3}{1}$ indicated that each note value was reduced to a third of its normal (previous) value, or that three notes of the $\frac{3}{1}$ were now to be performed in the time of one of the ¢ $o = \square\cdot$.

The $\frac{3}{2}$ indicated that each note value was reduced to $\frac{2}{3}$ of its normal value, or that three notes of the $\frac{3}{2}$ were now to be performed in the time of two of the ¢ $o \, d \, o \cdot$. The down-beat had a value of two measure beats in the fast triple time. The up-beat occurred on beat three:

$$ \frac{3}{1} \underset{1.\ 2.\quad 3.}{\downarrow\ \uparrow} \ \Big\| \ \frac{3}{2} \underset{1.2.\quad 3.}{\downarrow\ \uparrow} \ \Big\| $$

Before attempting an evaluation of tempi used in sixteenth-century music, a general rule in regard to tempo is in order:

Tempo is generally adjusted to the small note values in a piece of music, i.e., a speed permitting the clear articulation of such note values. Hence, the pieces in triple meter using only white note values and occasional pairs of quarter notes, or no black note values at all, were more likely to require a fast tempo. On the other hand, pieces in triple meter containing all note values would have a slower tempo, the whole note in the triple time being equal to the whole note in ¢, more or less. (See Ex. 226.)

The uniformity of the notation in the music of the sixteenth century points to the general acceptance of tempo stability. While there was a great deal of inconsistency in the use of time signatures, there is no doubt that a certain uniform temporal value was given to the tactus and that the only way of changing the time value of a given note was by proportions.

The practical tempo for this music seems to lie between M.M. 48–64 for the whole note in duple (¢) time.†

---

* See Arnold Schering, *Aufführungspraxis Alter Musik*, page 28.

† See Apel: *The Notation of Polyphonic Music 900-1600*, page 193.

The following tempi have been found adequate:

$\mathbb{C}\ o$ = M.M. 48. $\flat$ = 96   (Ex. 22).
$\frac{3}{1}$⊨· = M.M. 48 o = 144   (Ex. 109).
$\frac{3}{2}\ o$· = M.M. 24 $\flat$ = 72   (Ex. 143).
$\frac{3}{2}\ o$· = M.M. 32 $\flat$ = 96   (Ex. 230).

The tempo of the Hosanna on page 230 would undoubtedly be too slow with M.M. 48 as the norm; hence M.M. 64 is indicated, or M.M. 32 for two whole notes.

The location of suspensions in $\frac{3}{1}$ and $\frac{3}{2}$ mostly is on the second or the third beats:

Prep. Susp. Res.   or   Prep. Susp. Res.
  1   2   3   2   3   1

They occur, in most cases, before cadences. According to Jeppesen,* a change to large meter ($\frac{3}{1}$) causes the suspensions to be placed on the correct beats. Compare the Hosannas (Ex. 109 and 230).

Due to the fast tempo, half notes may be used as lower and upper auxiliaries and passing tones on the off beat in $\frac{3}{1}$ time. Quarter notes usually occur in pairs, corresponding to eighth notes, on the off beat. In $\frac{3}{2}$ time only the quarter note may be a passing tone (on the off beat); this applies to the lower and upper auxiliaries as well. No accented passing tone dissonances are permitted in triple time of this type.

2. Tollite jugum meum (Ex. 226). In the transposed Dorian mode.

The time signature is Φ (tempus perfectum diminutum), indicating the ternary mensuration of the brevis. The approximate tempo: M.M. 48. For the application of contrapuntal devices see Chapter 29.

Section 1.

1a: Tollite jugum meum
1b: Super vos dicit Dominus

Section 2.

Et discite a me, quia mitissum et humilis corde

Section 3.

Jugum enim meum suave est

Section 4.

Et onus meum leve.

Notice the reiteration, in Section 2, of the words "and learn of Me, because I am meek and humble of heart."

A complete thematic and harmonic analysis should be done by the student.

* Jeppesen: *Counterpoint*, translated by Glen Haydon, page 250.

Chapter 52.

The Mass

T‌HE most important musical parts of the Catholic High Mass are five in number and constitute the Ordinary of the Mass:

1. Kyrie eleison.
2. Gloria.
3. Credo.
4. Sanctus-Benedictus.
5. Agnus Dei.

These musical numbers occur in every Mass in the same order. In addition there is a complementary group of texts or music called the Proper of the Mass, the text and the music of which are chosen according to the Church Calendar. The complete order follows:

1. Introit (Proper)
2. Kyrie (Ordinary)
3. Gloria (Ordinary)
4. Prayer (Proper)
5. Epistle (Proper)
6. Gradual (Proper)
7. Alleluia or Tract, with sequence (Proper)
8. Gospel (Proper)
9. Credo (Ordinary)
10. Offertory (Proper)
11. Secreta (silent prayer)
12. Preface, chanted (Proper)
13. Sanctus-Benedictus (Ordinary)
14. Canon, Consecration (Ordinary)
15. Agnus Dei (Ordinary)
16. Communion (Prayer sung by priest)
17. Ite Missa est (Dismissal)

The polyphonic pieces used for the Proper are the Motets.

In the sixteenth century four distinct types of the polyphonic Mass may be recognized:

1. The Choral Mass, in which the thematic material in all movements was drawn from corresponding Gregorian chants.

Examples of this type of Mass: Morales *De Beata Virgine* (included in its entirety, with the Gregorian chant, in Peter Wagner's *Geschichte der Messe*, Vol. 1, p. 457), and Palestrina's *Mass for the Dead*.

2. The Cantus-firmus Mass, in which the same thematic material (Gregorian chant or original secular melodies) were used and usually placed in the tenor. Later types alternated the location of the Cantus-firmus between the parts (Palestrina's Mass *Ut Re Mi Fa Sol La* and *L'Homme Armé*).

3. The Transcription Mass, also called the Parody Mass.

It was general practice in the sixteenth century to make use of already existing compositions of both religious and secular character for the composition of Masses. The procedure in the adaptation of the musical material to the text of the different movements of the Mass varied. At times the whole composition was used without any change, but more often the material appeared in modified form.

Examples: Palestrina's Mass *Vestiva i Colli* (Ex. 22), based on his madrigal of the same name, and the Mass *Dies Sanctificatus*, on the motet (Ex. 140).

4. Masses with original thematic material.

The originality of the themes is sometimes open to doubt. The use of secular themes was forbidden after the Council of Trent, but the composers hid the circumvention of edict under titles such as *Sine Nomine*, etc. Apel mentions Palestrina's *Missa Brevis* under this heading.

The complete Latin text (see the English translation in Ex. 239) of the Ordinary of the Mass:

1. Kyrie eleison, Christe eleison, Kyrie eleison.

2. Gloria in excelsis Deo. Et in terra pax hominibus bonae voluntatis. Laudamus te. Benedicimus te. Adoramus te. Glorificamus te. Gratias agimus tibi propter magnam gloriam tuam. Domine Deus, Rex coelestis, Deus Pater omnipotens. Domine Fili unigenite Jesu Christe. Domine Deus, Agnus Dei, Filius Patris. Qui tollis peccata mundi, miserere nobis. Qui tollis peccata mundi, suscipe deprecationem nostram. Qui sedes ad dexteram Patris, miserere nobis. Quoniam tu solus sanctus. Tu solus Dominus. Tu solus Altissimus, Jesu Christe. Cum sancto Spiritu, in gloria Dei Patris. Amen.

3. Credo in unum Deum. Patrem omnipotentem, factorem coeli et terrae, visibilium omnium, et invisibilium. Et in unum Dominum Jesum Christum, Filium Dei unigenitum. Et ex Patre natum ante omnia saecula. Deum de Deo, lumen de lumine, Deum verum de Deo vero. Genitum, non factum, consubstantialem Patri: per quem omnia facta sunt. Qui propter nos homines, et propter nostram salutem descendit de coelis. Et incarnatus est de Spiritu Sancto ex Maria Virgine. Et homo factus est. Crucifixus etiam pro nobis; sub Pontio Pilato passus, et sepultus est. Et resurrexit tertia dia, secundum Scripturas. Et ascendit in coelum: sedet ad dexteram Patris. Et iterum venturus est cum gloria, judicare vivos et mortuos: cujus regni non erit finis. Et in Spiritum sanctum, Dominum, et vivificantem: qui ex Patre, Filioque procedit. Qui cum Patre, et Filio simul adoratur, et conglorificatur: qui locutus est per Prophetas. Et unam sanctam catholicam et apostolicam Ecclesiam. Confiteor unum babtisma in remissionem peccatorem. Et expecto resurrectionem mortuorum. Et vitam venturi saeculi. Amen.

4. Sanctus, Sanctus, Sanctus, Dominus Deus Sabaoth. Pleni sunt coeli et terra jloria tua. Hosanna in excelsis.

5. Benedictus qui venit in nomine Domini. Hosanna in excelsis.

6. Agnus Dei, qui tollis peccata mundi: miserere nobis. Agnus Dei, qui tollis peccata mundi: miserere nobis. Agnus Dei, qui tollis peccata mundi, dona nobis pacem.

THE MUSICAL TREATMENT OF THE MASS IN THE LAST PART OF THE SIXTEENTH CENTURY

Both polyphonic and homophonic style was used according to the length of the text of the different parts:

Kyrie eleison *Christe eleison* *Kyrie eleison*	Polyphonic. In three movements with different thematic material in each.
Gloria	Because of the longer text polyphonic and homophonic treatment alternated. The movement was usually divided in two parts: Part 1, Et in terra Part 2, Qui tollis.
Credo	Homophonic and polyphonic. Part 1, Patrem omnipotentem Part 2, Crucifixus Part 3, Et in Spiritum.
Sanctus	Polyphonic and homophonic. The movement is sometimes continuous (mostly in four parts): Ex. 44. Two parts: Sanctus and Hosanna, Ex. 66. Three parts: Sanctus, Pleni sunt, Hosanna, Ex. 112. The Hosanna is often in triple meter and in homophonic style.
Benedictus	Polyphonic. The number of voice parts is, as a rule, smaller by one than the other movements. The Hosanna is usually repeated after the Benedictus.
Agnus Dei. 1.	Polyphonic.
2.	Polyphonic. An extra voice part is often added.

Chapter 53.

Counterpoint in More Than Four Parts • Double and Triple Chorus

THE full development of the vocal polyphonic style of the sixteenth century was reached in the compositions for five or more parts. In these compositions, including the polychoral works, contrapuntal diversity was strictly maintained in all parts.

An important principle for writing many-voiced compositions is the proper observance of the use of rests. The full quota of voices should be employed for a certain percentage of time only, and during the course of the piece the number of voices should be varied.

FIVE-PART WRITING

The procedure is similar to that of four parts. One of the voice parts is doubled, most frequently the tenor, and imitated at the unison.

Preliminary exercises in five parts without text may follow the scheme outlined in the assignment for Chapter 50. For the setting of texts any of the five-part compositions in *Examples* will serve as models. The three offertories on pages 168, 172, and 177 are especially suitable.

SIX-, SEVEN-, AND EIGHT-PART WRITING

More freedom in the use of hidden octaves and fifths is now permitted, as well as parallel octaves and fifths in contrary motion. The possibilities of varied vocal color through the use of different combinations of voices should be exploited. The skill in this field is apparent even in the compositions for four voices, notably the Magnificat (Ex. 76).

Compositions recommended for analysis:

Palestrina: Mass *L'Homme Armé*; Agnus Dei (Ex. 120)
Mass *Ut Re Mi Fa Sol La* (Ex. 185)
Motets *Virgo prudentissma* (P. Vol. 1, part 1, p. 152)
Maria Virgo (P. Vol. 1, part 2, p. 158)
Tu es Petrus (P. Vol. 1, p. 146)

DOUBLE AND TRIPLE CHORUS

Polychoral composition is said to have originated in Venice. Conditions peculiar to St. Mark's Church, i.e., the possession of two organs and the division of the choir into two groups, may warrant such an assumption. The composer whose style adapted itself to these conditions was Giovanni Gabrieli, first organist of St. Mark's

Church from 1586 to 1612. His compositions are characterized by a varied use of combinations of voices and organ and brass instruments, resulting in colorful and dramatic antiphonal effects. The polychoral idea soon found its way to other musical centers, notably to the Roman School in the person of Palestrina.

The following works by Palestrina are recommended for analysis:

Double chorus: O, admirabile commercium (Ex. 131)
Stabat Mater dolorosa (P. Vol. VI, p. 96)
Laudate Dominum omnes gentes (P. Vol. II, p. 164)
Triple chorus: Laudate Dominum in tympanis (Ex. 123)
Nunc dimittis servum tuum, Domine (P. Vol. VI, p. 44).

In these compositions the possibilities in the use of purely vocal color and the maintenance of polyphonic style in each part are exploited with the greatest skill. Imitation is used to some extent, alternating with free treatment and sections in homophonic style.